Down with Anxiety!

DOWN WITH
ANXIETY!

LARRY KENNEDY

BROADMAN PRESS
Nashville, Tennessee

4282–56

Dewey Decimal Classification: 158

Subject headings: STRESS (PSYCHOLOGY) // WORRY

Library of Congress Catalog Card Number: 78–062537

Printed in the United States of America

Contents

1
Down with Anxiety!

When the angels appeared to announce the birth of Christ, they said: "I bring you good news of great joy that will be for all the people" (Luke 2:10, NIV). The emphasis was on joy, a joy that would fill the hearts of all people. The angels' message was that all those who would come to comprehend the significance of the birth of Christ would enter into a new joy. Do you have joy filling your heart?

Psychologists report that for many people Christmas is the most depressing time of the year. When I first read that statement, I found it difficult to believe; nevertheless, it is true.

Even for Christians, Christmas can be a time of anxiety. Psychologists call Christmas the "Holiday Paradox." More suicides occur during the first week in January than in any other week of the year. At Christmastime professional counselors find themselves besieged with people in various degrees of depression. Christmas should be the happiest time of the year; in reality, it has become for many the most depressing. This is true in both the Christian and the secular environment.

I can readily see why a nonbeliever would be depressed most of the time, but it seems to me that continual depression in the Christian community is a contradiction. The Bible teaches that a believer in Christ has joy filling his heart. My everyday experiences, though, seem to indicate that this is not true. Has the Bible lied to us? Are joy and

peace myths even for the believers? Do we have to live in
a perpetual state of anxiety?

The Problem of Anxiety

At this hour nonbelievers are not really impressed with
our kind of Christianity. They see no need for Christ because,
in most Christian communities, the Christians are no different from the non-Christians. The nonbeliever is defeated,
and he knows that this same spirit prevails in most Christians. The Christian community gives little evidence of being
victorious in the difficult circumstances of life. Anxiety is
as rampant in the church as it is in the secular community;
yet the Bible makes it clear that the believer does not have
to live in this abode of depression. The Scriptures contend
that the man in Christ has the power to defeat depression
and anxiety. Christ came to Bethlehem to fill men with
the reality of God. Man is to be the victor, not the victim.

If we were to give our honest testimonies as believers,
they would probably be extremely disturbing. Many of us
would have to confess unhappiness and defeat. We would
probably contend that our states of depression are the re-
sults of the *circumstances* in which we find ourselves. We
have convinced ourselves that circumstances produce our
anxieties, and we are hoping that God will change our
circumstances.

Some of you are thinking at this very moment that if
the rest of us were in your particular circumstance, we too
would be unhappy and defeated. You see your circumstance
as the cause of your anxiety and depression. Your reasoning
goes about like this: "If you had been rejected by a loved
one as I have been rejected, you too would be depressed."
Maybe your thinking runs in this vein: "If your children
had disappointed you as mine have disappointed me, you
would truly know depression." It could be that you are thinking, "If you had to live and work in my environment, you
would understand depression."

Some of you are convinced that the physical sickness you are having to endure is causing your depression. We could go on for several hours listing what we believe to be genuine circumstances that justify our anxieties. But listen to this: Although circumstances may initiate our anxieties, our mental attitudes will determine whether or not we remain in a state of anxiety. The mental attitude that always leads to anxiety and depression is *self-pity*. Self-pity, worry, and fear—not circumstances—are the causes of most anxiety and depression.

The Cause of Anxiety

The Bible offers evidence that self-pity, rather than circumstances, produces most of our anxieties. Consider the experience of Moses, as recorded in Numbers 11:10–15: "Then Moses heard the people weep throughout their families, every man in the door of his tent: and the anger of the Lord was kindled greatly; Moses also was displeased. And Moses said unto the Lord, Wherefore has thou afflicted thy servant? and wherefore have I not found favour in thy sight, that thou layest the burden of all this people upon me? Have I conceived all this people? have I begotten them, that thou shouldest say unto me, Carry them in thy bosom, as a nursing father beareth the sucking child, unto the land which thou swarest unto their fathers? Whence should I have flesh to give unto all this people? for they weep unto me, saying, Give us flesh, that we may eat. I am not able to bear all this people alone, because it is too heavy for me. And if thou deal thus with me, kill me, I pray thee, out of hand, if I have found favour in thy sight; and let me not see my wretchedness" (Num. 11:10–15).

Moses was a preacher with problems. From the moment he left Egypt, he heard nothing but complaints from the Hebrews. Every time Moses turned a corner, he was confronted with a complaint. Like people today, the Hebrews found something wrong with the preacher, the music director, the choir program, the youth program, and the budget. They were never pleased, and they constantly let Moses know it.

Finally, Moses was ready to give up. With gripes and complaints ringing in his ears, he begged of God, *"Kill me."* In this circumstance, Moses was depressed; in fact, he was depressed to the point of despair. He was in a mental state that modern psychology would call clinical depression. Moses' circumstances did not cause his anxiety; his attitude *in* the circumstance caused his depression. Moses was indulging in self-pity, anger, and bitterness. Rather than living by faith in God, he was living within himself. Moses took his eyes off the Lord of power and put his eyes on his circumstances. Moses was filled with anxiety and depression; but his despair was because of his self-pity, not because of his circumstances.

Think about the experience of Elijah as recorded in 1 Kings 19: "Ahab told Jezebel all that Elijah had done, and withal how he had slain all the prophets with the sword. Then Jezebel sent a messenger unto Elijah, saying, So let the gods do to me, and more also, if I make not thy life as the life of one of them by to-morrow about this time. And when he saw that, he arose, and went for his life, and came to Beer-sheba, which belongeth to Judah, and left his servant there. But he himself went a day's journey into the wilderness, and came and sat down under a juniper tree: and he requested for himself that he might die; and said, It is enough; now, O Lord, take away my life; for I am not better than my fathers. And he said, I have been very jealous for the Lord God of hosts: for the children of Israel have forsaken thy covenant, thrown down thine altars, and slain thy prophets with the sword; and I, even I only, am left; and they seek my life, to take it away" (vv. 1–4,10).

Having previously defeated the four hundred prophets of Baal, Elijah's fleeing the wrath of a domineering woman seems completely out of character. Elijah decided that Jezebel was greater and stronger than his Lord. As he fled, he experienced deep anxiety. The prophet informed the Lord that he alone stood faithful (self-pity). Of course, this was not true because seven thousand men like Elijah had refused to bow before Baal (1 Kings 19:18); but when a man is depressed, he cannot see beyond himself. Locked away in a cave on Mount Horeb, the prophet almost drowned in tears of self-pity as he asked the Lord to take his life. Elijah's anxiety was *not caused by his particular circumstance;* his anxiety was the natural outgrowth of his mental attitude—an attitude of self-pity, anger, and fear.

Job knew the experience of depression. He lost his children, his wealth, and his health. His wife told him to "curse God and die." The last straw came when his friends informed him that all his problems were caused by some sins that he had refused to confess. In desperation Job cried out, "Let the day perish wherein I was born, and the night in which it was said, There is a man child conceived. Why died I not from the womb? why did I not give up the ghost when I came out of the belly?" (Job 3:3,11). If we had been in Job's place, our responses would probably have been quite similar. This truth is clear—as difficult as his circumstance was, Job's anxiety was not caused by his circumstance. His attitude of self-pity brought him to the dismal pit of despair.

The prophet Jeremiah gave his life to the preaching of God's word, but his pleading fell upon deaf ears. The people refused to listen, and they rejected Jeremiah and his message. He was mocked and ridiculed. The prophet discovered that even members of his own family had plotted against him. Having been rejected by all, the prophet lamented, "Cursed be the day wherein I was born: let not the day wherein my mother bare me be blessed. Cursed be the man who brought tidings to my father, saying, A man child is born unto thee; making him very glad. And let that man be as the cities which the Lord overthrew, and repented not. Wherefore came I forth out of the womb to see labour

and sorrow, that my days should be consumed with shame?"
(Jer. 20:14–16,18). Like the prophets before him, Jeremiah
regretted the day that he had been born. He was a deeply
depressed man; but we must realize that Jeremiah's depression was not caused by his circumstance. The prophet was
defeated by his mental attitude.

A Cure for Anxiety

Anxiety is a universal problem, and its cause is usually
rooted in self-pity; the Bible offers a cure for anxiety. Part
of this cure is found in 1 Thessalonians 5:18. If we can learn
to put the words of Paul into practice, we can defeat the
attitude of self-pity and, in the process, whip the common
colds of mental illness—anxiety and depression. Paul said,
"In every thing give thanks: for this is the will of God in
Christ Jesus concerning you" (1 Thess. 5:18).
   Self-pity is a habit. If we are to defeat this blight of the
soul, then we must enter into a new habit—give thanks
in *every circumstance.* Paul said *in every thing give thanks.*
This admonition is not qualified. No conditions are hedged
around it. No exceptions are made. We are told that God
expects us to be thankful in all situations. No matter how
difficult the circumstance may be, we are to give thanks
(see Eph. 5:20). In this verse we find *one* of the keys to defeating anxiety. A man who is thanking God in every circumstance of life is a man who is defeating self-pity.
   At first our reaction to this concept is one of disbelief;
yet if we will believe and practice what the apostle said,
our lives will be revolutionized. We will enter into the joy
of which the angel spoke when he announced the birth of
Christ.
   Paul not only preached thankfulness in every circumstance, but he also put his preaching into practice. In life
he demonstrated that circumstances do not have to destroy
us. In Acts 16 Luke related that Paul and Silas were placed
in jail for preaching the gospel. All evidence pointed to a

quick execution. Because of the tragic circumstances, Paul and Silas could have complained. Having given their lives to missions, they could have doubted the justice and mercy of God; instead, the account states: "At midnight Paul and Silas prayed, and sang praises unto God: and the prisoners heard them" (Acts 16:25).

What were these men doing? They were thanking God. Paul had learned a truth that Moses, Elijah, Job, and Jeremiah had failed to recognize. Circumstances do not keep us in a state of anxiety; our mental attitude locks us into anxiety. Paul believed "that all things work together for good to them that love God, to them who are the called according to his purpose" (Rom. 8:28). Because he believed this truth, he could thank God in all things. He knew that God's resources were always available to him. He knew that God could bring good out of bad situations, and he refused to drown in anxiety.

Notice carefully that the prisoners heard Paul and Silas singing praises to God (Acts 16:25). Can you imagine their shock? Surely they were amazed that men in such a circumstance could be so positive in outlook. This verse drives home the truth that thanking God in all things is not only healthy for us, but is also healthy for all those around us. God uses our thankfulness to help others break the self-pity habit. *Our faith has its highest expression when we thank God in all things.* To pray with a thankful heart is to have the faith attitude, and it is the faith attitude that will destroy the tyranny of anxiety.

God never intended for us to dwell in the house called anxiety. He wants us to believe "that all things work together for good to them that love God." Our confidence in that Bible truth is demonstrated when we "in every thing give thanks." Can you accept the challenge to start thanking God in all things? Acceptance has nothing to do with feelings; it is a matter of faith. You cannot wait until you feel like it to thank God. Do not live by your feelings; instead, *live by faith* and defeat self-pity and anxiety.

2

What Do You See— the Mud or the Stars?

2 Corinthians 11:23–29

Through examples from the Word of God and contemporary living, I challenge you to live by the faith attitude. This attitude is always expressed in prayer, forgiveness, love, and positive thinking. The person who allows these traits to dominate his life will never be a victim; he will always be a victor. Whenever the faith attitude is exhibited, depression and despair are hard to find.

Circumstances are not the keys to a happy life. If you are waiting for a certain set of circumstances to occur before you experience happiness, you will never have happiness. Your *attitude* determines whether or not you are victorious in life. Man's greatest need is not a new set of circumstances; his greatest need is a new attitude—a new way of *thinking*.

If your life is controlled by worry, failure, fear, anger, self-pity, bitterness, and resentment, life will be difficult for you. If any of these traits are in your thinking pattern, you will spend most of your time as a depressed, defeated, and unhappy person. Anger, self-pity, fear, and resentment are certainly the ingredients for a miserable life. If you allow these negative attitudes to control your mind, you will be like a sinking ship in a bottomless ocean.

When we first hear that attitude, not circumstance, is the key to mature living, we instantly rise in anger. We do this for the simple reason that we do not like to admit that *self* is the major problem. It is so much easier on the ego to blame our problems on our circumstances; but if we are going to live positive and worthwhile lives, we must come to grips with our attitudes. If you will change your thinking from negative (worry, self-pity, failure, fear, anger, resentment) to positive (faith, love, forgiveness, optimism), you will alter your life-style from negative to positive, from unhappiness to happiness, from defeat to victory, from anxiety to optimism. Remember the biblical words "As a man thinketh, so is he" (Prov. 23:7). How and what are you thinking?

Consider the words of Paul in 2 Corinthians 11:23–29. In this text Paul described the circumstances of his life, and this Bible text is a basis of demonstrating again the fact that attitude (the way you think), not circumstance, is the key to victorious living.

Concerning himself, Paul said, "I have worked much harder, been in prison more frequently, been flogged more severely, and been exposed to death again and again. Five times I received from the Jews the forty lashes minus one. Three times I was beaten with rods, once I was stoned, three times I was shipwrecked, I spent a night and a day in the open sea, I have been constantly on the move. I have been in danger from rivers, in danger from bandits, in danger from my own countrymen, in danger from Gentiles; in danger in the city, in danger in the country, in danger at sea; and in danger from false brothers. I have labored and toiled and have often gone without sleep; I have known hunger and thirst and have often gone without food; and I have been cold and naked. Besides everything else, I face daily the pressure of my concern for all the churches. Who is weak, and I do not feel weak? Who is led into sin, and I do not inwardly burn?" (NIV).

Many years ago two men were placed in prison. One prisoner was dejected and depressed; the other was full of faith and hope. One prisoner felt that all was lost, and he was ready to give up. The other prisoner refused to give up; he believed that one day he would be set free. The optimist pondered the difficulty that he and his companion were in;

then he wrote, "Two of us look through the bars: one sees the mud; the other sees the stars." The two men were in the same circumstances, but their attitudes were miles apart. The difference in the two was not in the circumstances but in how they viewed the circumstances. There was a difference in attitude.

Paul spent much of his ministry in the mud. In fact, some of his enemies saw to it that his nose was literally kept in the mud. Most of the time Paul lived in most difficult circumstances, but he refused to see the mud. He always looked to the stars because his attitude was that of faith and hope. Out of the most tragic and horrible circumstances, he could write, " 'We are considered as sheep to be slaughtered.' No, in all these things we are more than conquerors through him who loved us" (Rom. 8:36–37, NIV). Paul refused to allow self-pity, worry, anger, bitterness, and resentment to dominate his life. He never fell victim to his circumstances because he lived by the faith attitude. To the apostle every difficult and tragic circumstance was a trial whereby God would be glorified and his own faith would be made stronger. Paul was victorious in life, not because of his circumstances but because of his attitude.

What is your attitude? What fills your mind? If you will share your attitude, I can tell you how you are getting along in life.

While riding a train, a minister observed a handsome elderly couple. The wife was dressed in furs and diamonds and was the envy of all the other women on the train, but her disposition did not match her appearance. She constantly complained about everything. She criticized the food, the service, and the railway car.

Her husband, who was striking in appearance, was a calm, considerate man. As his wife raved about the abominable service, he sat calmly, occasionally showing embarrassment at his wife's attitude. In an attempt to change the tone of the conversation, the husband engaged the minister in a conversation in which they discussed their occupations. Finally the husband said with a grin on his face, "My wife is in the manufacturing business."

This surprised the minister because the wife certainly did not seem to be the executive type. The minister asked, "What does your wife manufacture?"

"Unhappiness," her husband replied. "She manufactures her own unhappiness." Like so many others, she saw only the mud.[1]

What are you manufacturing? If your attitude is that of self-pity, anxiety, anger, bitterness, or failure, you are manufacturing depression and unhappiness. Do not blame your attitude on your circumstance. Do not allow your particular circumstance to become a catalyst for the self-pity attitude. Allow faith, forgiveness, and love to fill your mind. Be a daily reader of God's Word, and let prayer be a way of life. If you will do this, you will discover that life is exciting and rewarding, no matter what the circumstance.

Dr. Harold Wolff, editor in chief of *Archives and Neurology and Psychiatry,* read a paper entitled "A Scientific Report on What Hope Does for Man." In this paper Dr. Wolff discussed the experiences of the 31,000 Allied soldiers imprisoned in Japan and Korea during World War II. Dr. Wolff stated that of the 31,000 soldiers who were imprisoned, 8,000 died. Most of these men died not because of the difficult living conditions and inhumane treatment, but because of their negative attitudes. The soldiers who saw only the mud were filled with self-pity and despair; these men literally wasted away. The other prisoners, though, were filled with faith and hope; they chose to see the stars. The difference in the two groups was not the circumstance (they all had the same circumstance); the difference was in attitude.

What is your attitude? Do you see the mud, or do you see the stars? Are you filled with self-pity and anxiety, or are you filled with faith and hope? The answer to this question determines whether life for you will be defeat or victory.

Dr. David Tsutada was a Japanese Christian living in Japan at the outbreak of World War II. Because of his Christian beliefs, the Japanese authorities placed him in prison. He spent the duration of the war in a dark, filthy, damp prison cell. He was compelled to live on bread and water, and his weight eventually dropped to seventy pounds. Dr. Tsutada refused to indulge in self-pity. Neither did he become angry with those who had mistreated him. In the isolated confines of his cell, he began to make plans for a Bible school that he would establish if he were ever released. In the avenues of his mind, he began to imagine every detail of the school. With his imagination he built the buildings, worked out a curriculum, hired the faculty, and enrolled his children. Eventually Dr. Tsutada was released, and today he operates one of the outstanding Christian schools in Japan.

What enabled this man to accomplish so much? Was it his circumstance? Certainly not. His circumstance was horrible. The difference was in his attitude of faith. If he had spent his days in prison feeling sorry for himself, he probably would have died. He exchanged the self-pity anxiety attitude for the faith attitude. He refused to see the mud; he looked to the stars.

The question is not what our circumstances are. We must ask what our attitudes are in the midst of our circumstances.

I believe the words of Dr. S. I McMillen are worth repeating at this point:

> Our attitude of mind is a most important factor in determining whether we shall suffer from exposure to life's daily stress. Our tendency in the past has been to blame our diseases on the people around us instead of blaming our troubles on our faulty reaction [attitudes] to those people. The sorrows and insults of daily living need not cause much trouble if we take them with the right mental attitude. Chronic brooding over sorrows and insults indi-

cates faulty adaptation, which can cause any condition from itching feet to insanity. The most common form of faulty reaction is self-pity . . . . Our attitude decides whether stress makes us better or bitter.[2]

Ralston Young made his living carrying luggage in Grand Central Station in New York City. Because of his Christian spirit, he became one of the best-known workers at the station. He used every opportunity to share his faith with those around him. On one occasion he was asked to help a lady in a wheelchair. He sensed that she was very sad and depressed. He noticed that she was wearing a lovely dress, and he instantly commented on her striking appearance. His remark appealed to her, and she brightened up. Finally the woman asked, "Why are you being so kind to me?"

Young told the lady that he had sensed that she was not feeling well, and he hoped that he could bring a little joy into her life. The lady replied that it was difficult for her to be happy because she was in constant pain, and at times the pain was unbearable. She then asked Young, "Do you have any idea what it means to be in pain all the time?"

Young responded, "Yes, ma'am. I do know what it means to be in pain. I lost an eye many years ago, and at times it still burns like a hot iron. But I have discovered that prayer makes a difference. Prayer does not remove the pain, but it gives me the strength to bear the pain."

A year later the daughter of the crippled lady found Young in Grand Central Station. She shared with Young how her mother, before her death, had been helped through the simple philosophy that he had offered. She stood before Young with big tears rolling down her cheeks. Young watched quietly for a while and then said, "Don't cry, missy; don't cry. Be thankful to God. Many people have become orphans much younger than you. You had your mother for a long time. You will see her again. She is near to you now, and she will always be near to you."

Ralston Young had the attitude that we all need. He refused to see the mud, no matter how difficult the circumstance; he always saw the stars. He had learned at an early age that attitude is far more important than circumstances.

In my previous church there is a lady who daily demonstrates the power of the faith attitude over difficult circumstances. Miss Devear Jones lives alone in her apartment. She has no close relatives and is completely dependent upon the church. She is severely handicapped because she is almost totally blind. She exists in what all of us would describe as a very difficult circumstance; however, she is a person filled with faith and thanksgiving. If you are ever depressed, I would encourage you to visit Miss Jones. She will greet you with a smile and bring joy to your heart. Recently some ladies of our church carried her to a hospital in Memphis for surgery. During the trip she related that one of the happiest Christmases she had ever experienced was during a convalescence in a hospital. Miss Devear has that blessed attitude whereby she refuses to see the mud and seeks only to see the stars. She has exchanged the self-pity attitude for the faith attitude.

Earlier I shared Paul's personal testimony concerning the difficult and tragic circumstances he had faced as a Christian missionary (2 Cor. 11:23–29). I believe Paul's attitude toward such circumstances is best described in Romans 8:31–37. Paul said: "What, then, shall we say in response to this? If God is for us, who can be against us? He who did not spare his own Son, but gave him up for us all—how will he not also, along with him, graciously give us all things? Who will bring any charge against those whom God has chosen? It is God who justifies. Who is he that condemns? Christ Jesus, who died—more than that, who was raised to life—is at the right hand of God and is also interceding for us. Who shall separate us from the love of Christ? Shall trouble or hardship or persecution or famine or nakedness or danger or sword? . . . . No, in all these things we are more than conquerors through him who loved us" (NIV).

Paul's ministry is a continuous echo of the fact that attitude, not circumstance, is the key to victorious living. We are challenged through the power of God's Spirit to exchange the self-pity attitude for the faith attitude. Choose today to ignore the mud and see the stars. You will never regret such an exchange.

3
Your Attitude May Be Killing You

Ephesians 4:30–32

Circumstances may initiate anxiety and depression, but our attitudes determine whether or not we remain defeated. Those who live by the anger attitude are going to be depressed persons. Anger not only puts us into a state of depression but it also leads to ulcers, heart attacks, and other destructive ailments. Dr. S. I. McMillen, in his book *None of These Diseases,* has said, "What a person eats is not as important as the bitter spirit, the hates, and the feelings of guilt that eat at him. A dose of baking soda in the stomach will never reach these acids that destroy body, mind, and soul." Concerning the relationships between anger and disease, Dr. McMillen said,

> A study at one hospital revealed, through personal interviews with patients suffering from mucous colitis, that resentment was the most prominent personality characteristic occurring in ninety-six percent of the victims . . . . In life's frog ponds, perhaps we are able to out-croak our fellows, but it might truthfully be written on many thousands of death certificates that the victims died of "grudgitis." We have heard people say, with clenched teeth, "I'll get even with that skunk if it's the last thing I ever do." Too often it is exactly that.[1]

When Jesus said that we were to forgive seventy times seven, he gave us good spiritual advice; he also gave us good medical advice. When we replace anger with forgiveness, we are saving our bodies from ulcers, heart attacks, colitis, toxic goiters, high blood pressure, and numerous other diseases. Anger leads to despair and physical destruction.[2]

As we consider the anger attitude, look at this negative attitude in three ways: the definition of anger, the destructive nature of anger, and the deliverance from anger.

The Definition of Anger

In Ephesians 4:30–32 the Bible states, "Grieve not the holy Spirit of God, whereby ye are sealed unto the day of redemption. Let all bitterness, and wrath, and anger, and clamour, and evil speaking, be put away from you, with all malice: And be ye kind one to another, tenderhearted, forgiving one another, even as God for Christ's sake hath forgiven you." Paul tells us not to grieve the Holy Spirit through anger. The word *grieve* means to pain, to hurt, to cause sorrow. When the believer allows anger and bitterness to rule his life, God is hurt. The indwelling Holy Spirit is affected by the anger attitude of the believer. When the Spirit of God is grieved, he is unable to do his work in our lives.

In the statement found in Ephesians 4:30–32, we have five words that embrace the concept of anger. Paul gave us several definitions or expressions of the anger attitude. The first word that he used is bitterness. The Greek word is *piknia,* which means resentfulness or harshness. The bitterness attitude is defeating many people; the resentful heart is the unhappy heart. The second word used by Paul in this context is wrath. The Greek word is *thumos,* and it brings to mind a sudden burst of anger. This is the type of anger that quickly subsides. The third Greek word used by the apostle to depict anger is *arge,* which describes anger that continually boils and has its end in revenge. Next Paul used the word clamour. *Krauge,* the Greek word, indicates an expression used by Paul in this context as *evil speaking.* The Greek word *blasphemica* refers to slanderous speech that has as its purpose personal injury. All of these Greek words—*piknia, thumos, arge,* and *krauge*—are expressions of the anger attitude. In Colossians 3:8 Paul used these same words to describe the anger attitude that is to be removed. The Colossian expression "be put away from you" refers to the taking off of old clothes that need to be discarded. The anger attitude, said Paul, is like old clothes that must be thrown into the garbage dump and burned.

The Destructive Nature of Anger

Having defined anger as it is seen in the Bible, we need to notice carefully the destructive nature of anger. As previously stated, anger is destructive in both the physical and spiritual realm.

From the physical standpoint, the anger attitude is a sure way to destroy your body. For instance, let us take the example of John Smith. John was a very likable fellow, provided he did not lose his temper. When one of his fellow workers failed in an assignment, John became furious and used the sharpest words he could find; however, the abuse always backfired because John always ended up in bed, a very sick man. His wife would be forced to call the doctor because John was vomiting his life away. If you were to see John Smith, you would feel sorry for him. His eyes are bloodshot, and he desperately needs help. He has spent a fortune on medical services, all because of his anger.

For John Smith this is only the beginning of future misery. Since his stomach is not made of steel, his ulcers will eventually have ulcers. Because of his anger, toxic hormones are being thrown into his bloodstream, affecting every vital organ in his body. John Smith will die long before his time because of his attitude. Dr. McMillen has said:

> Running people down does not keep us free from a host of diseases of body and mind. The verbal expression of animosity toward others calls forth certain hormones from

the pituitary, adrenal, thyroid, and other glands, an excess
of which can cause disease in any part of the body.[3]

When a grizzly bear is eating, he will not allow any other
animal near him except the skunk. The skunk can come
and go as he pleases, as far as the grizzly is concerned. A
grizzly never attacks a skunk because he knows the high
price he would pay for getting even. It is a tragedy that
we do not have the common sense of a grizzly bear. When
we indulge in anger, we are going to pay a high price in
mental and physical health.

An old lady of about eighty years was informed by the
doctor that her blood pressure checked out at 230. With
an expression of concern the doctor said, "Your blood pressure is up today."

The little old lady smiled and said, "That's understand-
able. I just had a heated argument with another lady in
the waiting room."

If we live by anger, we also pay a heavy price in the
spiritual realm. As previously stated, anger grieves the Holy
Spirit. Any time that we grieve the Spirit, our lives are
outside the will of God; thus, no good can come from that
relationship.

Anger is a sin, and it has the power to lead us into more
sin. When anger rules our hearts, there is no end to the
spiritual chaos that can come into our lives.

The Deliverance from Anger

A minister gave up the pulpit to become a doctor. When
asked why he had done this, he responded, "I took up the
practice of medicine because I discovered that people will
pay more to care for their bodies than for their souls." Some
years later this same man became a lawyer. When asked
why he changed professions for a second time, he responded,
"I took up the practice of law because I discovered that
people will pay more money to get their own way than for

either body or soul." There is much truth in this story. As someone has said, "Worthwhile is the saying that a man is a fool who can't be angry, but a man is wise who won't be angry."

In Ephesians 4:32 Paul gave us the road map that will deliver us from the anger attitude: "Be ye kind one to another, tenderhearted, forgiving one another, even as God for Christ's sake hath forgiven you." This contains the key to deliverance because God has forgiven us of all our sins, and he gives us the strength to forgive those who have wronged us.

We are keenly aware of personal insults and injury. Every time we are insulted or persecuted, we should view the experience in two ways. *First,* we should see the experience as a means to grow in God's grace. We cannot grow in love and forgiveness unless our lives are put to the test. Every insult is really a God-given opportunity to grow in Christ-likeness. *Second,* we must remember that every time we are ridiculed and insulted, God is giving us the opportunity to show that Christ really can make a difference in the human life. If we counter an insult with anger and resentment, we are simply saying, as Christians, that Christ really does not make a difference. The anger attitude in the life of a believer denies the reality of the indwelling Christ. Many people today do not believe that Christ can make a difference in life because they see many Christians who are angry, bitter, and resentful persons. Too often we are like James and John who wanted to call down fire upon the Samaritan village because the Samaritans would not give them lodging (Luke 9:52–56).

In Acts 7 we meet a unique personality called Stephen. The Bible tells us that Stephen was filled with the Holy Spirit. God was in control of his life, and he demonstrated the reality of God's fullness. Because of his beliefs, Stephen was taken outside the city gates and stoned to death. As he received the blows from the hurled stones, he looked to heaven and said, "Lord, lay not this sin to their charge" (Acts 7:60). Rather than being filled with anger, Stephen was filled with God's forgiveness. The attitude of forgiveness was not wasted because the Bible tells us that Paul witnessed that death. Paul saw that Christ could make a difference in a human life. Undoubtedly this experience played an important part in his conversion.

What is your attitude? Are you angry, bitter, resentful? If you are, then we both know that you are defeated and having a difficult time in life. How tragic it is that we justify our anger by calling it righteous indignation. Ninety-nine percent of the time, righteous indignation is nothing more than sinful anger. Anger will only make us sick in every area of our lives. We must confess our anger to God. We must ask him to take it away and, in its place, to give us the attitude of forgiveness. This is the only way to live successfully.

Dr. William Sadler, in his book *The Practice of Psychiatry*, has made the following observation:

> No one can appreciate so fully as a doctor the amazingly large percentage of human disease and suffering which is directly traceable to worry, fear, conflict . . . unwholesome thinking, and unclean living. The *SINCERE* acceptance of the principles and teachings of Christ with respect to the life of mental peace and joy, the life of unselfish thought and clean living, would, at once, wipe out more than half the difficulties, diseases, and sorrows of the human race. In other words, more than one half of the prophylactic power of actually giving up the personal and practical spirit of the real teachings of Jesus. The teachings of Jesus applied to our modern civilization—understandably applied, not merely nominally accepted—would so purify, uplift, and vitalize as that the race would immediately stand out as a new order of beings, possessing superior mental power and increased moral force. Irrespective

of the future reward of living, laying aside all discussions
of future life, it would pay any man or woman to live
the Christ-life just for the mental and moral rewards it
affords here in this present world. Some day man may
awake to the fact that the teachings of Christ are potent
and powerful in preventing and curing disease. Some day
our boasted improvement may indeed catch up with the
teachings of this man of Galilee.[4]

It is amazing that, in our day, the scientific community
is accepting the full teachings of Jesus Christ and holy Scripture. May the layman in the pew have the same foresight.
The way of victorious living is before us. With the right
attitude—the attitude of forgiveness—life will be an adven-
ture in complete living. God's Spirit can open our minds
to the attitude of forgiveness.

4
Your Thinking May Be Hazardous to Your Health

Ephesians 4:29–32

Self-pity and worry are attitudes that always lead to depression. Most of us justify our condition of self-pity and worry by magnifying the circumstances that we are experiencing. We usually blame the outward circumstances of life for our state of depression, but life has demonstrated too many times that a negative mental attitude is really the key to despair. The antidote for self-pity and worry is a faith that is expressed in praise, prayer, forgiveness, and love. Creative faith can always deal with the circumstances of life. The apostle Paul and other biblical personalities have demonstrated repeatedly under extremely difficult circumstances that a person does not have to live in defeat and depression. These men turned from self-pity and anxiety, no matter how difficult the circumstance; and they lived by faith in Christ.

Consider another mental attitude that leads to depression—our expressions of anger, bitterness, and hatred. It seems to me that anger and self-pity are really tied together. Anger is a response to an offense or a personal injury; and anger is also, in reality, an expression of self-pity. Most of the time when we are bitter, we are feeling sorry for ourselves. *Self* is the problem. Naturally, when we indulge in self-pity, we will be depressed.

The Bible fully recognizes the role of anger in defeatist living. This is one reason why the Spirit of God warns against harboring anger in the heart. Angry, bitter, resentful people are miserable human beings. They get no joy from life and are unable to give joy to others. Even some Christians, strange as it may seem, are known for their anger and bitterness.

As we consider the attitude of anger and the cure for it, notice Ephesians 4:29-32: "Do not let any unwholesome talk come out of your mouths, but only what is helpful for building others up according to their needs, that it may benefit those who listen. And do not grieve the Holy Spirit of God, with whom you were sealed for the day of redemption. Get rid of all bitterness, rage and anger, brawling and slander, along with every form of malice. Be kind and compassionate to one another, forgiving each other, just as in Christ God forgave you" (NIV).

According to this passage, being insulted or offended is no excuse for indulging in anger, bitterness, or malice. The Word of God is very clear in calling the believer to repudiate the anger attitude and to live by the forgiving attitude (which is an expression of faith in Christ).

The Cause of Anger

The cause of anger is not complicated. We hate to say the word but we must—SELFISHNESS. It is not easy to face the truth that our bitterness has its roots in selfishness. Although we love to excuse our sins and justify them to ourselves as we nurse our hurts and indulge in angry, vengeful feelings, they are all motivated by selfishness. When I am angry, it is because someone has violated my rights, and I am interested in myself. When I am bitter against someone, it is because he has done something against me. Vengeance is always inspired by selfishness.[1] Dr. S. I. McMillen, in his book *None of These Diseases,* expresses it this way:

One may ask, "Isn't it foolish to give up our rights?" Perhaps it is not foolish, since in giving up our rights we insure our own happiness. In giving the other fellow "a

piece of our mind," we always lose our peace of heart.
. . . It is the spirit of retaliation that calls forth glandular
toxins, and man suffers from his strong sense of self-ex-
pression and self-pity. If one takes time to analyze the
cause of faulty adaption to life's difficulties, one will often
discover a little four letter word—*self.* Stress and disease
result because of our unwillingness to sacrifice the big
"I."[2]

To say that selfishness is the cause of anger is to agree
with the Bible that sin is evident in all of us.

The Cost of Anger

Emotionally, we pay a heavy cost for anger and bitterness.
The anger attitude always puts a person in the dismal abyss
of despair and defeat. In a state of anger, it is usually said
of a person, "He is not himself." How true that is. Anger
toward one person always affects our emotions toward others. If we are angry with a man, we discover that it is difficult
to love the members of our families; the anger and the bitterness of the day always go home with us.

When we indulge in anger and bitterness, we pay a heavy
price mentally. Dr. McMillen has said:

The moment I start hating a man, I become his slave. I
can't enjoy my work any more because he even controls
my thoughts. My resentments produce too many stress
hormones in my body and I become fatigued after only
a few hours of work. The work I formerly enjoyed is now
drudgery. Even vacations cease to give me pleasure . . . .
The man I hate hounds me wherever I go. I can't escape
his tyrannical grasp on my mind. When the waiter serves
me porterhouse steak with French fries, asparagus, crisp
salad, and strawberry shortcake smothered with ice
cream, it might as well be stale bread and water. My
teeth chew the food and I swallow it, but the man I hate
will not permit me to enjoy it . . . . The man I hate may

be miles from my bedroom; but more cruel than any slave driver, he whips my thoughts into such a frenzy that my innerspring mattress becomes a torture rack.[3]

Anger has its social consequences. No one wants to be around a bitter, angry person. Those folks who are noted for their disgruntled attitudes are always weeded out of the fun times of life. No one desires to spend time with an angry person.

Physically, the cost of anger is devastating. Doctors and medical associations are now contending that from 60 to 90 percent of man's bodily illnesses are emotionally induced. The leading culprits in this sickness are anger and fear. Someone has asked, "How can our emotions (anger) cause physical illness?" Our physical bodies are tied directly to our nervous systems. When the nervous system becomes tense through anger, it adversely affects all parts of the body.

Anger and bitterness have much to do with producing ulcers and other stomach disorders. When you clench your fist, your fingers turn white because the flow of blood has been restricted to that area. When you release your grip, the fingers return to the natural color as the blood is able to flow freely. Stretched across a person's stomach is a muscle that is emotionally controlled; during a fit of anger this muscle will tighten and restrict the flow of blood to the vital organs of the heart, stomach, liver, intestines, lungs, and gallbladder. One psychologist has said that 97 percent of the people who have ulcers have them because of anger. When this doctor discovers that the patient has an ulcer he always asks, "Who has made you angry?" The doctor stated that after that question the patient becomes angry with him.

Many people, at this very moment, are wondering why God has permitted sickness to invade their lives. It is obvious from the new insights of medicine that, in most cases, God did not will it. Rather, personal anger—sin—caused it.

If you allow bitterness, anger, jealousy, malice, and envy to have a place in your life, you will die before your time. If you do not experience an early death, you will spend most of your years as a very sick person. Someone has said that we do not have much to say about how we look at sixteen, but we certainly can determine how we are going to look at sixty.

Anger has a spiritual cost. Angry and bitter Christians have a difficult time loving God. This is true because they cannot love and forgive others. On more than one occasion, Jesus said that our love for him was always expressed in love for others. The Bible states, "If a man say, I love God, and hateth his brother, he is a liar: for he that loveth not his brother whom he hath seen, how can he love God whom he hath not seen? And this commandment have we from him, That he who loveth God love his brother also" (1 John 4:20–21).

Angry Christians also doubt their salvation. Jesus understood this clearly when he revealed a portion of the Lord's Prayer. He said, "Forgive us our sins, just as we have forgiven those who have sinned against us" (Matt. 6:12, TLB). Jesus made it very clear that God's forgiveness of our sins is in direct proportion to our willingness to forgive others. Please note that if you indulge in anger and resentment, your fellowship with Christ will always be shaky.

An angry Christian is a Christian who is grieving the Holy Spirit. Our Bible text makes it clear that anger and all of its other forms grieve the Holy Spirit. The Greek word for grieve means to cause sorrow or pain. We bring sorrow to God's heart when we indulge in anger. When God is grieved, his power cannot work in our lives; we become powerless and ineffective Christians.

The Christian who lets bitterness rule his life pays a terrible cost in the spiritual realm. Many believers were never used of God because they never confessed or turned from the sin of anger (bitterness, envy, malice, resentment).

The Cure for Anger

There is a cure for anger and bitterness. Since the Bible teaches us to rid ourselves of anger, it is obvious that anger can be dwelt with permanently. In Ephesians 4:31 the Bible says, "Get rid of all bitterness" (NIV). This expression refers to the casting away of old clothes. Anger and malice are like old clothes that need to be taken off and thrown away. Let us consider several principles that will help us rid ourselves of the anger attitude.

First, anger must be faced as a sin and confessed to the Lord. Until we admit the truth that bitterness is a sin, anger will always be a problem in our lives. You may have to confess the sin of anger ninety-nine times a week, but there has to be a beginning. Anger is a habit as well as a sin. Let us face it and deal with it now. The promise of the Bible is, "If we confess our sins, he is faithful and just and will forgive us our sins and purify us from all unrighteousness" (1 John 1:9, NIV).

Second, if you are offended or insulted by someone, always realize that your sins against God are far greater than any sins committed against you. We must see the magnitude of our sins against God. Once we come to understand the forgiveness that God offers us, we shall be more willing to forgive those who have sinned against us. If God has forgiven us (and he has if we are believers), surely we can forgive others who have insulted us. No sin against you is as great as your own personal sins before the Lord. Paul was making this plea in Ephesians 4:32 when he said, "Be kind and compassionate to one another, forgiving each other, just as in Christ God forgave you" (NIV). The parable of the unmerciful servant in Matthew 18:21–35 is stating the same principle.

Third, when you are offended by another, always remember that the problem belongs to God and not to you. Listen to Paul in Romans 12:17–19: "Do not repay anyone evil for evil. Be careful to do what is right in the sight of everybody. If it is possible, as far as it depends on you, live at peace with everyone. Do not take revenge, my friends, but leave room for God's wrath, for it is written: 'It is mine to avenge, I will repay,' says the Lord" (NIV).

Fourth, when you are offended, begin to thank God. Remember the commandment of 1 Thessalonians 5:18, "In everything give thanks," and put it into practice. You can be thankful for personal insults for two reasons. First, the offense gives you the opportunity to grow in the character of Christ. The only way to grow in love and forgiveness is to put it into practice in difficult situations. When you are offended, God is giving you the opportunity to grow in Christ-like character.

A classic example of this idea is seen in the Bible personality Joseph. The record in the book of Genesis reveals that Joseph had more than his share of personal insults; yet he never became an angry, bitter man. He never brooded over his personal injuries, and God molded him into a man of great character. When Joseph revealed himself to his brothers in Egypt (the same brothers who had sold him into slavery), he said, "Therefore be not grieved, nor angry with yourselves, that ye sold me hither: for God did send me before you to preserve life. So now it was not you that sent me hither, but God" (Gen. 45:5,8). Joseph practiced forgiveness. He viewed all of his problems as an opportunity to grow under the leadership of God. In all the personal offenses, he saw the hand of God at work for good.

A man's spiritual maturity is not determined by how many people he never offends. *Spiritual maturity is determined by how he responds when he is offended.* The spiritual person is one who exercises love and forgiveness in the face of personal injury and insult. The immature Christian is the person who is constantly telling everyone how he has been offended or injured. As a pastor I have come to see that some of my ministry has been spent brooding over personal offenses. In the problems of life, God has been seeking to mold my character into Christlikeness. On many occasions I have refused to be molded.

God has given us an opportunity to demonstrate that Jesus Christ really does make a difference in a believer's life. Every time we exercise love and forgiveness in the face of a personal offense, we are saying to the person who has offended us and to all who are watching: *Christ really does make a difference.* He does give spiritual strength in every situation. Has it ever occurred to you when you were insulted, or when a member of your family was offended, that God was giving you the opportunity to demonstrate the uniqueness of the Christian life by expressing forgiveness? Beginning today, let us realize that the insults which come to us and our families are, in reality, opportunities whereby we can show that Christianity really works.

Anger has a cause and the cost is terrific—but, praise God, it can be cured. When anger is replaced with the attitudes of love and forgiveness, all of life assumes a new dimension.

Tim LaHaye in his book *Spirit-Controlled Temperament* gave the following illustration, which is an ideal summary of this discussion:

> A lovely Christian lady came to my study to tell me her side of the problems in her home. When I confronted her with the fact of her angry, bitter spirit, she blurted out in her defense, "Well, you'd be angry too if you lived with a man who constantly ran roughshod over you and treated you like dirt!" Admittedly, he was not treating her the way a Christian man should, but her reaction could not possibly be caused by generosity; instead, it was plain old selfishness. The more she indulged in her selfish-

ness and let anger predominate, the worse her husband treated her.

I confronted her with the fact that she had two problems. She looked at me rather startled and asked, "Did I hear you correctly—I have two problems? I only have one, my husband." "No," I said, "you have two problems. Your husband is one problem, but your attitude toward your husband is another. Until you as a Christian recognize your own sin of selfishness and look to God for a proper attitude, even in the face of these circumstances, you will continue to grieve the Holy Spirit of God." The change in that woman in almost one month's time was almost unbelievable. Instead of using her husband as an excuse to indulge in anger, she began to treasure her relationship to Jesus Christ more than the indulgence of her own selfishness. She went to Him who has promised to "supply all your needs according to His riches in glory by Christ Jesus" and began to experience victory over bitterness, wrath, anger, and all those emotional attitudes that grieved the Holy Spirit. Instead of waiting for a change in her husband's behavior, she literally changed her husband's behavior by hers. She told me that when God gave her victory over her own reaction to his miserable disposition, she began being kind to the one who was "despitefully using her," just as our Lord had instructed. Since love begets love and we reap what we sow, it was not long before the husband began to respond with kindness.[4]

Anger always leads to misery. With the help of God, put bitterness and malice out of your life. You will never regret making that decision.

5
The Waste of Worry

Matthew 6:25–34

John Doe always worried about everything. His associates all knew him as a continuous worrier. One day Bill Smith was walking down the street when he saw his worrying friend bouncing along as happy as a man could be. John Doe was actually whistling and humming and wearing a huge smile. He looked as if he did not have a care in the world. Bill Smith was amazed by the transformation that had occurred, and he had to know what had caused this change in attitude.

Bill stopped John Doe and asked, "John, what has happened to you? You do not seem worried anymore. I never saw a happier man in my life."

John replied, "A wonderful change has occurred in my life. I have not worried about anything in many months."

Bill Smith was thrilled to hear the good news and asked, "How did you ever get this change in attitude?"

John Doe replied, "You see, I hired a man to worry for me."

Bill Smith smiled and asked, "Well, how much does he charge to worry for you?"

"A thousand dollars a week," answered John Doe.

With a disdainful look, Bill Smith asked, "How could you possibly raise a thousand dollars a week?"

"I don't know," said John. "That's his worry."

All of us, at one time or another, have wished for someone to help us carry the burden of all our problems. It is the message of biblical revelation that God is seeking to help

us in all our problems. The Bible tells us to cast all our
cares upon him because he cares for us (1 Pet. 5:7). Most
of the time we refuse the wisdom of God and simply worry
about things that we cannot control, and worry always leads
to despair. Worry is an attitude of the mind; it is a way
of thinking about life. It is negative thinking that adversely
affects the emotions of man. Anytime a man is emotionally
unstable, his physical body will deteriorate. Jesus understood the destructive power of worry, and he knew that
this negative mental attitude was detrimental to man's
health. He commanded men not to worry and offered an
alternative attitude.

Ponder the words of Jesus as recorded in Matthew 6:25–
34: "Therefore I tell you, do not worry about your life, what
you will eat or drink; or about your body, what you will
wear. Is not life more important than food, and the body
more important than clothes? Look at the birds of the air;
they do not sow or reap or store away in barns, and yet
your heavenly Father feeds them. Are you not much more
valuable than they? Who of you by worrying can add a
single hour to his life? And why do you worry about clothes?
See how the lilies of the field grow. They do not labor or
spin. Yet I tell you that not even Solomon in all his splendor
was dressed like one of these. If that is how God clothes
the grass of the field, which is here today and tomorrow
is thrown into the fire, will he not much more clothe you,
O you of little faith? So do not worry, saying, 'What shall
we eat?' or 'What shall we drink?' or 'What shall we wear?'
For the pagans run after all these things, and your heavenly
Father knows that you need them. But seek first his kingdom
and his righteousness, and all these things will be given
to you as well. Therefore, do not worry about tomorrow,
for tomorrow will worry about itself. Each day has enough
trouble of its own" (NIV).

The Greek word for worry, *merimnan,* literally means
to divide, part, rip, or tear apart. Some scholars translate

this word as to divide the mind or to go to pieces. It is certainly an accurate description of worry. When a man goes to pieces, he is never involved in creative action and purpose; instead, he simply divides his mind and puts ulcers on the lining of his stomach.

Are you worrying? Is your mind divided? Are you going to pieces?

Joseph Fort Newton, a pastor for many years in Philadelphia, used to write a column of spiritual advice in one of the local newspapers. In October of 1964 *Reader's Digest* reprinted one of his articles. The distinguished pastor said in his article:

> For many years I conducted a newspaper feature, "Everyday Living," which reached millions of people. Out of the mountains of letters, not more than a half dozen ever brought up any question of theology . . . . The first thing that these letters show is that private enemy number one in human life is neither sin or sorrow; it is fear. The one most rife is fear of ourselves, and this is not healthy. Men today fear failure, breakdown, poverty—fear lest they be unequal to the demands made upon them. So few have any material security; and we have set so much store on such security that the lack of it assumes hideous forms and gigantic dimensions in the night, robbing us of the rest needed to do our work. It is this self-fear which makes life an agony. Next to fear—if not a form of it—is the nagging, gnawing worry which wears us out, and unfits us for living. Worry is like slow poison . . . . Unless it is checked, it cuts a channel into which all other thoughts are drained.[1]

Newton said worry had to be checked. In Matthew 6 Jesus told us how to check worry. If your mind is divided, three truths are paramount in your life. *First,* you are sinning against God because worry is a sin. If Jesus said not to worry, and we worry, then we are sinning against God.

Second, if you have set up housekeeping with worry, you are depressed and fearful. Every neuron in your psyche is fatigued. *Third,* if you are worrying, your health is in serious jeopardy. You are in the process of tearing down every cell in your body. You are becoming everything that a child of God should not be. Thank goodness, Jesus told us how to deal with worry. In these verses of Matthew 6, Christ told us to exchange the worry attitude for the faith attitude. He calls us to change our thinking.

Jesus calls us to see three truths as we break the worry habit: the worth of our lives, the waste of worry, and the way of God.

The Worth of Your Life

If you and I are to have victory over worry, a new thought is going to have to be embedded in the cells of our minds— the worth of our lives to God. When we worry we are saying, whether we realize it or not, that God is not really interested in our needs. We act as if we stand alone against the devil and his angels. Worry is an expression of faithlessness.

God is deeply interested in our needs. He understands us better than anyone because he made us. He loves us with a love that cannot be measured in human understanding. Please put it down in the tablets of your mind that God loves and cares for you. You are not alone; in fact, he knows how many hairs are on your head.

To stress the worth of our lives, Jesus said that since God gives life, he can be trusted for the lesser things to support life: "Therefore I tell you, do not worry about your life . . . . Is not life more important than food, and the body more important than clothes?" (Matt. 6:25, NIV). In the words of William Barclay, "If anyone gives us a gift which is beyond price, surely we can be certain that such a giver will not be mean, . . . and careless, and forgetful about much less costly gifts."

To impress upon his listeners the worth of man's life to

God, Jesus used the illustration of the birds. Jesus said, "Look at the birds of the air; they do not sow or reap or store away in barns, and yet your heavenly Father feeds them. Are you not much more valuable than they?" (Matt. 6:26, NIV). Birds are not lazy. If you have ever watched birds build a nest or feed their young, you know that birds are diligent workers. They work, but they do not worry. They live one day at a time, and God meets their daily needs. If God is interested in meeting the needs of the birds, surely he is interested in us. We are more valuable than birds because we were made in the image of God.

I vividly remember the Christmas when I received my first BB gun. Within hours after having received the gun, I killed my first bird. When I brought the trophy home, my sister cried for hours. It broke her heart to see me kill the birds. More than once she asked me, "How would you like it if the birds had BB guns and could shoot back?" In some ways, God has the same attitude toward the birds that my sister did. If he cares for the birds, surely he cares for us.

To illustrate our worth and value to God, Jesus referred to the flowers of the fields. Jesus said, "See how the lilies of the field grow. They do not labor or spin. Yet I tell you that not even Solomon in all his splendor was dressed like one of these. If that is how God clothes the grass of the field, which is here today and tomorrow is thrown into the fire, will he not much more clothe you, O you of little faith?" (Matt. 6:28–29, NIV).

The lilies of the field were the scarlet poppies that bloomed for only one day on the beautiful hillsides of Palestine. When the flowers ceased to bloom, women gathered them and used them as fire material for the cooking ovens; nevertheless, God still clothed the flowers in a beauty that far surpassed the splendor of Solomon. The beauty was for only one day, yet God honored the flowers. If God gives such beauty to a short-lived flower, surely he will care for man. Jesus was simply saying that if God values the flowers, surely we know that he values us.

Let us not worry. God knows our needs. He loves us, and our lives are priceless in his sight. By an act of our wills and in his strength may we exchange the worry attitude for the faith attitude.

The Waste of Worry

If we are to have victory over worry, we must come to understand the waste of worry. If worrying helped, I believe that Jesus would have advocated the worry attitude; but as Jesus knew, the worry attitude is destructive to the human personality.

To show the waste of worry, Jesus asked a question, "Who of you by worrying can add a single hour to his life?" (Matt. 6:27, NIV). Worrying does not increase the life span; it really shortens it.

Worry produces emotional stress, which may account for two-thirds of the physical illness today. High blood pressure, heart trouble, kidney disease, goiter, arthritis, headaches, and strokes are just some of the physical problems that can be produced by the worry attitude. According to one doctor, worry places more stress on the heart than any other stimulus, including physical exercise and fatigue. When you worry, your adrenal gland is functioning so rapidly that your bloodstream cannot throw off the excessive adrenaline. Jesus was correct. When you worry, you cut your life span in half.

Worry is a waste because it really expresses a lack of faith in God. As Jesus scrutinized the worry attitude of the disciples, he said to them, "O you of little faith." Could it be that the worry attitude so prevalent among Christians is one reason that lost people are not impressed with Christianity? Since the worry attitude is an expression of a lack of faith in God, the Lord is not able to work out his will in our lives when we worry. God can only work where there is faith.

The Way of God

The worry attitude can be defeated if we follow the way of God. Jesus said, "Seek first his kingdom and his righteousness" (NIV). Simply put, we are to put our faith in God and not in ourselves. We are to trust the Lord even when we do not feel like it. We are to live by faith and not by our feelings. We are saved by faith. How difficult it is to learn that we also *live* by faith! Faith is the key that takes us through the abyss of worry and out of the smog of despair. Paul said that he could do all things through Christ, who gave him strength (Phil. 4:13). If the living Christ could do that for Paul, he can and will do it for us; however, this promise of grace is conditioned upon our willingness to put our faith in him.

Whatever problem you have, in faith turn it over to the Lord. Begin first by thanking God for the problem. Do not be shocked by such an admonition. It is based upon Scripture. Paul said, "Give thanks in all circumstances, for this is God's will for you in Christ Jesus" (1 Thess. 5:18, NIV). He also wrote: "Always giving thanks to God the Father for everything" (Eph. 5:20, NIV). Why is it that giving thanks in all things is so important? Giving thanks to God in *all* things is one of the highest expressions of faith a man can offer to God. (Anyone can thank God for *good* things.) We can give thanks in all things because the Bible says, "All things work together for good to them that love God" (Rom. 8:28). Even from the most tragic circumstance in the life of the believer, God is able to bring good.

In Philippians 4:6–7 there is a wonderful promise given to those who take all their problems to God in thankful prayer: "Do not be anxious about anything, but in everything, by prayer and petition, with thanksgiving, present your requests to God. And the peace of God, which transcends all understanding, will guard your hearts [emotions] and your minds [mental attitude] in Christ Jesus" (NIV). What a marvelous promise! When you exchange the worry attitude for the faith attitude, the peace of God takes over your mind and heart. But this only occurs when you begin—by faith, not feelings—to thank God in all things.

Worry is a sin that always leads to unhappiness. The Lord is calling us to trust him in every circumstance.

One day a gentleman said to a beggar, "God give you a good day, my friend."

The beggar answered, "I thank God I never had a bad one."

Said the gentleman, "God give you a happy life, my friend."

The beggar responded, "I thank God I am never unhappy."

In amazement the gentleman cried, "What do you mean?"

The beggar smiled and said, "When it is fine, I thank God. When it rains, I thank God. When I have plenty, I thank God. When I am hungry, I thank God. Since God's will is my will and whatever pleases him pleases me, why should I say I am unhappy when I am not?"

The gentleman asked, "Who are you?"

Replied the beggar, "I am a king."

"Where is your kingdom?" cried the gentleman.

Quietly the beggar said, "In my heart."

Long ago the prophet Isaiah said, "Thou wilt keep him in perfect peace, whose mind is stayed on thee: because he trusteth in thee" (Isa. 26:3).

In whom do you trust?

6
Do You Worry About Your Worry?

Philippians 4:4–8

The January 8, 1973 edition of *Newsweek* magazine made the following statement concerning depression at Christmas:

> This is the time of year when the affliction cuts deepest in those who are prone to it: The holidays are over, gone, and the bright promise of Christmas, often painfully unfulfilled, has given way to the bleak reality of the winter that lies ahead. Psychiatrists' telephones jangle with calls for help. An executive oppressed by the incessant gabble of his children has begun drinking heavily. A young housewife, physically exhausted by weeks of anticipatory tension, by gift buying and meal planning, suddenly finds herself in the grip of insomnia. A widow, alone in a small apartment, is racked by protracted fits of sobbing. Now the days are gray, the nights long and spring is far away. . . . The holidays are organized to guarantee disappointment.[1]

The article in *Newsweek* discussed at length the problem, as well as the probable causes, of depression. It concluded with this statement: "Clearly, there is no magic formula to relieve depression. And the debate over how to deal with the pervasive and destructive malady will grow more intense as the research effort into depression gathers momentum."

Many pastors also believe there is no magic formula in dealing with depression; however, I believe the Bible offers a spiritual formula for depression and anxiety. The authors of the Testaments saw self-pity, worry, fear, and anger as the cause for most despair. The prophets of the Testaments were concerned about mental health because they believed that God was concerned about it. They gave spiritual answers in dealing with negative thinking. Even in the most difficult and tragic circumstances, the biblical writers believed that man was able to rise above the circumstances and escape being defeated by them. In the thinking of the prophets, circumstances did not lead to depression; rather, they believed that a man's mental attitude during the circumstance determined whether or not he would be depressed. They demonstrated this truth many times.

We know that mental attitudes affect our emotions and that our emotions affect our physical actions. If our mental attitudes are those of self-pity, worry, fear, and anger, we are going to be emotionally sick. If we are emotionally sick, then our everyday living will be warped and distorted. The key to wholesome living is a positive attitude. The Bible presents a positive attitude as an *attitude of faith in God.* The invitation of the Bible is to fill your mind with faith. What is filling your mind? What are you allowing to occupy your mind? What kind of thinking has set up housekeeping in your mind? Are you filled with self-pity, worry, and fear; or are you filled with faith? The answer to these two questions determines whether you are going to spend the rest of your days in depression or in happiness.

The apostle Paul stressed the importance of thanking God in all things (1 Thess. 5:18) as a means of dealing with depression. Thanking God in all things may be the highest expression of faith that a man can offer to God. This is the reason why thanksgiving gives us victory over our circumstances. To tell a man to have faith when his circumstances are difficult can be a very general answer to a problem; but when we give thanks in all things, our faith has a specific means of expressing itself. *Thanking God in all things is the highest expression of faith a man can offer to God.* We can thank God in all situations because we know that his resources are available in every situation.

We can simplify this thesis by reading Philippians 4:4–8. Paul was aware that self-pity, worry, and fear were attitudes of the mind that could hamper the spiritual life of a believer. When the mind is obsessed with self, depression is the product. In this text Paul gave an answer to worry (if this is not the same as self-pity, then they are "kissing cousins"); and, in so doing, he gave us an answer to depression.

The text reads as follows: "Rejoice in the Lord always. I will say it again: Rejoice! Let your gentleness be evident to all. The Lord is near. Do not be anxious about anything, but in everything, by prayer and petition, with thanksgiving, present your requests to God. And the peace of God, which transcends all understanding, will guard your hearts and your minds in Christ Jesus. Finally, brothers, whatever is true, whatever is noble, whatever is right, whatever is pure, whatever is lovely, whatever is admirable—if anything is excellent or praiseworthy—think about such things" (Phil. 4:4–8, NIV).

Paul told us to do four things in dealing with worry: practice praise, practice the presence of the Lord, practice prayer, and practice positive thinking. Let us consider his first command.

Practice Praise

Paul said, "Rejoice in the Lord always. I will say it again: Rejoice!" The answer to worry is faith in God, which expresses itself in praise. As we read this verse, let us remember that Paul was in prison as he wrote this letter (Phil. 1:12–14). He was in a Roman jail, with the sentence of death hanging over his head. If there was ever a circumstance conducive to depression, this was it. If circumstances give us the right to indulge in self-pity and unhappiness, then

Paul had a green light; yet this negative spirit was not seen in his life. He was a man whose mental attitude was that of faith. Faith filled his mind, and that faith was expressed in praise.

As Paul told his readers to rejoice always, he anticipated their disbelief. He knew how stubborn the human mind can be. No one wants to admit that he is his own worst enemy. We all want to blame our circumstances, rather than self-pity, for our misery. Anticipating disbelief in his command, he repeats it: "I will say it again: Rejoice!"

This rejoicing is in "the Lord" because only those in Christ will have the resources for such an experience. Our position in Christ is the basis for rejoicing, no matter what the circumstances. We are children of the King—rejoice!

Can people rejoice always? It depends upon our faith— our attitudes of mind. If we believe that Romans 8:28 is true, "that all things work together for good," then we can practice 1 Thessalonians 5:18: "In every thing give thanks."

Some people practice praise by singing. When they sense a desire to indulge in self-pity, they move by faith and begin to sing praises to God. If you are like me and cannot carry a tune, singing does not offer much hope. But I have found an answer in the reading of God's Word. You can practice praise by reading some of the great Psalms of the Old Testament. When you sense that you are in the arena of self-pity, read God's Word aloud.

Read Psalm 150: "Praise ye the Lord. Praise God in his sanctuary: praise him in the firmament of his power. Praise him for his mighty acts: praise him according to his excellent greatness. Praise him with the sound of the trumpet: praise him with the psaltery and harp. Praise him with the timbrel and dance: praise him with stringed instruments and organs. Praise him upon the loud cymbals: praise him upon the high sounding cymbals. Let everything that has breath praise the Lord. Praise ye the Lord."

Let us always remember Psalm 117: "O praise the Lord,

all ye nations: praise him, all ye people. For his merciful kindness is great toward us: and the truth of the Lord endureth for ever. Praise ye the Lord."

Fill your mind with praise thoughts; this is God's therapy to insure healthy living. I do not know the author of these praise psalms, but I certainly know that he was not indulging in self-pity. As you fill your mind with God's Word, you will discover that despair has difficulty in possessing your heart.

Remember that we are not talking about feelings; we are talking about faith. If you wait until you feel like reading praise Scriptures, you probably will never read the Word of God. If the devil realizes that you live by your feelings, he will bombard you with negative feelings to prevent your acting by faith; but as you move by faith, the feelings will eventually come. Remember that we must live by faith, not by feelings.

Practice the Presence of the Lord

Paul gave us another answer to the problem of worry and self-pity. He said, "The Lord is near." As believers in Christ, we continually have the presence of Christ in our lives. There are several Scriptures that we must keep before us. Listen to Jesus in John 14:16–17: "I will ask the Father, and he will give you another Counselor, the Spirit of truth, to be with you forever . . . for he lives with you and will be in you" (NIV). The word *counselor* is the Greek word *paraclete.* It literally means one called in to help. As Christians we have the Holy Spirit, the actual presence of God, living in our lives. Jesus said that the indwelling Spirit comes in *forever;* we are not left as helpless children without guidance. No wonder Jesus could say with confidence, "Do not let your hearts be troubled and do not be afraid" (John 14:27, NIV).

Paul was right—the Lord is near. We are never alone. Our problems are his problems; our difficulties are his difficulties. He will live in our hearts forever. When we indulge in worry and self-pity, we act as if we were alone. We deny the words of Jesus. Let us begin now to fill our minds with the truth that our lives are indwelt by the Holy Spirit. No matter what our circumstance, God stands with us; the Lord is greater than our problems. Let us practice the presence of the Lord.

One day in Russia, during the persecution of the Christians by Stalin, the secret police arrested a group of Christians as they worshiped in a home. The arresting officer began to count heads as the Christians were ushered from the house. He announced to his associates that there were thirty believers in all. One of the Christians said, "That's not true. There are thirty-one." The arresting officer hurriedly recounted and, with indignation in his voice, announced that only thirty were present. The Christian calmly said, "No, sir, you are incorrect. There are thirty-one of us present at this worship service. You see, Jesus is here, too."

When Jesus ascended to his heavenly Father, he said, "And surely I will be with you always, to the very end of the age." We rest our lives upon that promise. We are never alone.

Practice Prayer

In Philippians 4:4–8 Paul presented precepts to practice for dealing with self-pity and worry. He had told us to practice praise and the presence of the Lord. Next he told us to practice prayer. The word *anxious* literally means to divide or separate. Paul said that we must not worry; we must not let our lives go to pieces. That's exactly what worry and self-pity do for a person. Mental activity that engages in worry always divides the mind, bringing havoc upon the human heart.

Paul said to practice prayer rather than engaging in worry. Notice that he mentioned prayer with *thanksgiving*.

Paul never left his thesis of thankfulness in all things. According to the apostle, we are not to worry about anything; but in everything, with thanksgiving, we are to present our needs to God. He told us that when we approach God in this manner, the reward is the peace of God which guards our hearts.

The word *guard* is a military word. It describes soldiers who have gathered around a person to offer complete protection and security. We can have God's protection when we go by faith in thankful prayer into his presence.

Is it really possible not to worry about anything? Can we, in faith, come to the place where our minds are never divided? Was Paul only offering wishful thinking when he wrote these words? Can a person thank God no matter what the circumstance may be? Corrie ten Boom, in her book *The Hiding Place,* tells of how faith in God upheld her through the pits of hell. Her testimony bears witness that thanking God in all things is the key to liberating a mind from self-pity. Miss ten Boom spent many months in a Nazi concentration camp. During this ordeal, she saw her sister and many other women die. However, she and her sister never despaired because they daily practiced 1 Thessalonians 5:18. Giving thanks in all things, even in a Nazi hellhole, was a way of life for them. Today her radiant Christian life is proof that there is spiritual power in that attitude.

Practice Positive Thinking

Whatever fills our minds affects our total lives. If your mind is filled with self-pity and worry, you are becoming a negative person. You are useless to yourself and to all those whose lives you touch. The truth of this hour is that no one has to live negatively. God wants to fill our minds with faith, and he waits now for us to open ourselves to his deity.

Long before Peale wrote *The Power of Positive Thinking,* the apostle Paul was sharing the same concept. He realized that a healthy life was the product of a healthy mind. If the mind is filled with faith in God, then the life radiates the reality of God. Listen again to the words of the apostle: "Finally, brothers, whatever is true, whatever is noble, whatever is right, whatever is pure, whatever is lovely, whatever is admirable—if anything is excellent or praiseworthy—think about such things." The Greek expression *think about* means more than meditation. This expression means to reckon or to take into account so that one's course of action is changed for the better. Fill your mind with wholesome thoughts, and your life will radiate the joy of the Lord.

Psychiatrist Dr. Karl Menninger said, "Attitudes are more important than facts." I would like to modify that statement by saying that attitudes are more important than circumstances. Any circumstance facing you, no matter how difficult and even seemingly hopeless, is not as important as your attitude toward the circumstance. If you fill your mind with a triumphant thought pattern, you will be a triumphant person. Whatever else we may say about faith, we must say that it is an attitude of the mind. What is your attitude?

Paul said that he could do all things through Christ, who gave him strength. The apostle had the victory over self-pity and worry because he practiced praise, God's presence, thankfulness in prayer, and positive thinking. The indwelling Christ gave him the strength to put these virtues into action. Christ did it for Paul, and the Lord will do it for you.

There was once a very small fellow who applied for a job as a woodsman in the Pacific Northwest. He approached the boss and asked for a job cutting wood. Because of his size, the boss and the other woodsmen began to laugh. They all decided to have a little fun. They told the small fellow that he could have the job, provided he would demonstrate his power with the ax. With the firm belief that the little fellow would make a fool of himself, the boss selected a huge tree for the test. The little man lifted his ax; and, with only one swing, the giant tree came crackling down. All the woodsmen were stunned and viewed the little fellow with disbelief. Finally the boss approached the little man and said, "Where did you ever learn to cut wood like that?"

The little fellow replied, "In the Sahara Forest."

The boss responded, "Don't you mean the Sahara Desert?"

The little man answered, "That's what they call it now."

Our circumstances vary. Some of us believe that our circumstances resemble trees too large to be cut down; however, for the Christian, this is not true. Approach every circumstance with the attitude of faith; put into practice the commands of Paul. You will be the victor, and self-pity and despair will never be able to park on your doorstep.

7

Are You a God,
or Are You a Worm?

Psalm 8

In a counseling session, a counselor asked a young mother to complete the sentence "I am . . ." ten times. Slowly the young mother replied,

"I am . . . a poor mother."

"I am . . . a disappointment to my parents."

"I am . . . overweight."

"I am . . . unhappy."

"I am . . . divorced."

The woman continued until she had listed ten negative things about herself.

The counselor then said, "I did not ask you to list ten bad things about yourself. I want you to try again, and this time I want you to list ten good things about yourself."

The woman replied that she could not. Eventually she said, "I try to be a good mother, and I try to keep a clean house."[1]

Many of us are like this young lady. We have a poor self-image. We feel worthless—of no value; there is no self-esteem in our hearts. Psychologists, psychiatrists, and pastors realize that when a person does not have a healthy self-image, he will be depressed and unhappy. When we are filled with negative self-evaluation, life will be one long trail of misery.

Dr. Maxwell Maltz, in his book *Psycho-Cybernetics*, has said:

The most important psychological discovery of this century is the discovery of the "self image." Whether we realize it or not, each of us carries about with us a mental blueprint or picture of ourselves. This self-image is our own conception of the "sort of person I am". . . . To really "live," that is to find life reasonably satisfying, you must have an adequate and realistic self image that you can live with. You must have a wholesome self-esteem. You must have a self that you can trust and believe in.[2]

In trying to build an adequate self-image, there are two extremes that we must reject. The first view that hinders a healthy self-image is found in humanistic philosophy and literature. The humanistic view of man tends to deify man. This view attempts to make man more than he is. History and the everyday experiences of man demonstrate that claiming deity for ourselves is not the answer in building a positive self-image. In the words of one author, "If we are so good, or if we are so capable of achieving our own perfection, why, after thousands of years, do we continue to cause and multiply such gigantic problems?"[3]

The other view that hinders the development of a purposeful self-esteem is found in religion. Most of us are familiar with John Newton's song:

> Amazing grace! how sweet the sound,
> That saved a *wretch* like me!
> I once was lost, but now am found,
> Was blind, but now I see.[4]

Isaac Watts wrote in a similar vein when he penned these words:

> Alas! and did my Saviour bleed,
> And did my Sovereign die,
> Would he devote that sacred head
> For such a *worm* as I?[5]

We can certainly appreciate the life out of which John Newton wrote his hymn. He had been a slave trader. But when he experienced the grace of God, he saw vividly the depths of his own sin. Isaac Watts wrote at a time when great emphasis was placed upon the holiness of God and the sinfulness of man. However, for many persons, expressions like *wretch* and *worm* have led to self-hate. If a person has experienced many failures, the concept of being a worm only adds to the misery.

Are you a god, or are you a worm? You are neither one. You are a human being, a person whom God loves very much. There are many blocks to use in building a healthy self-image. The first block is seeing ourselves as God sees us. In the Word of God we have the basis for a positive self-evaluation. If we can see ourselves as God sees us and take his view seriously and literally, we are on the right path to happiness.

The Bible speaks of man in three ways: the dignity of man, the deception of man, and the deliverance of man.

The Dignity of Man

The emphasis in the Bible is on the dignity of man. The prophets and authors of the Bible stress the worth and value of man to God. In Genesis 1:26–27 the Bible states, "God said, Let us . . . make mankind in Our image, after Our likeness; and let them have complete authority over the fish of the sea, the birds of the air, the . . . tame beasts, and over all of the earth, and over every thing that creeps upon the earth. So God created man in His own image, in the image and likeness of God He created him; male and female He created them" (AMP).

The Genesis account stresses that we are not accidents of God. From the beginning God was deeply interested in you and me. He created us with great care; then he put the stamp of himself upon us because we were created in his image.

In Psalm 8:1–6 we read: "O Lord, our Lord, how excellent (majestic and glorious) is Your name in all the earth! You have set your glory on the . . . heavens . . . . When I view and consider Your heavens, the work of Your fingers, the moon and the stars which you have ordained and established; What is man, that You are mindful of him, and the son of . . . man, that You care for him? Yet You have made him but little lower than God . . . , and You have crowned him with glory and honor. You made him to have dominion over the works of Your hands; You have put all things under his feet" (AMP).

Although we may not know the author of this psalm, we know that he did not have a poor self-image. He saw himself as a special creature in the universe of God, and he realized that he was important to the Lord. Like this psalmist, we must catch the picture that God has crowned us with glory and honor.

The Almighty created us and gave us a special place in his universe; however, the concern of the Lord did not stop at creation. He is deeply interested in us now. We are never misplaced; God is always aware of our needs, and daily he seeks to care for us. Listen to what Jesus said in Luke 12: 6–7: "Are not five sparrows sold for two pennies? Yet not one of them is forgotten by God. Indeed, the very hairs of your head are all numbered. Don't be afraid; you are worth more than many sparrows" (NIV).

When we fail in life, we sometimes believe that God has turned his back and left us on the ash heap. This is not the case. Even in our failures God loves us and seeks to heal our broken hearts. Our worth to God cannot be measured. He never abandons us to the island of despair. Let us begin now to see our own worth according to the revelation of God. If God is not willing to give up on us, surely we can have the same attitude.

The Bible stresses the dignity and value of our lives. The early church understood this quite clearly, and it was proclaimed in every village. Historian R. R. Palmer has said:

It is impossible to exaggerate the importance of the coming of Christianity . . . . Where the Greeks had shown man his mind, the Christians showed him his soul; and they taught that in the sight of God all souls were equal . . . . The Christians sought out the diseased, the crippled, and the mutilated to give them help. Love, for the ancients, was never quite distinguished from Venus; for the Christians, who held that God was love, it took on deep overtones of sacrifice and compassion.[6]

The Deception of Man

Just as the Bible stresses the dignity of man, it also stresses the deception of man. Man has a basic problem called sin. The Bible puts it this way: "God looks down from heaven upon the sons of men to see if there are any that are wise, that seek after God. They have all fallen away; they are all alike depraved; there is none that does good, no, not one" (Ps. 53:2–3, RSV). The prophet Jeremiah said, "The heart is deceitful above all things, and desperately corrupt; who can understand it?" (Jer. 17:9, RSV). The apostle Paul proclaimed, "For all have sinned and fall short of the glory of God" (Rom. 3:23, NIV). John summed it all up when he wrote, "If we say we have no sin, we deceive ourselves, and the truth is not in us" (1 John 1:8).

I believe the words of psychiatrist James D. Mallory, Jr., are worth repeating at this point. He said:

People often focus on sin, meaning bad behavior, as man's basic problem. But man's basic problem is self-worship, self-centeredness, egocentricity, whatever word you want to use for the I in the middle of sin. It is the big I that has led man away from God and into paths of his own choosing. . . . Man is a sinner because of his basic condition of self-centeredness.[7]

All of us have the problem of egocentricity. I remember that one of my seminary professors said that our problem is that we all want to play God. However, our tendencies to go our own ways do not mean that God does not care for us. While we fall short of God's standard, we are still of great value to God. The image of God upon our lives is always present. In fact, we are so valuable that God sent his Son to break the power of self-centeredness.

The Deliverance of Man

How do I know that we are of value to God? How do I know that God cares for us and is deeply interested in us? I know he cares because Christ came and died for our sins. Every child of God knows John 3:16: "For God so loved the world that he gave his only Son, that whoever believes in him should not perish but have eternal life" (RSV). Paul put it best when he said, "While we were yet helpless, at the right time Christ died for the ungodly. Why, one will hardly die for a righteous man—though perhaps for a good man one will dare even to die. But God showed his love for us in that while we were yet sinners Christ died for us" (Rom. 5:6–8, RSV).

God is interested in us. He has manifested his love for us in the person of Jesus Christ. As we acknowledge our egocentricities and turn from our selfish selves to God, the Spirit of God takes residence in our lives to give us his power to defeat sin. In the words of John R. W. Stott, "it is thus through His atoning death that the penalty of our sins may be forgiven; it is through His indwelling Spirit that the power of our sins may be broken."[8]

When we fail, there is the tendency to feel that God considers us worthless and that he has rejected us. May God help us to ignore our feelings and to rest upon the assurance of God's Word. The Bible declares that even though we have sinned, the Almighty loves us with an everlasting love. He loves us so much that he sends his Spirit to live in our hearts and to give strength for the problems of life.

In John 17 we have the high priestly prayer of Jesus. In that prayer Jesus prayed for you and me. Jesus said,

"I do not pray for these only, but also for those who believe in me through their word. I in them and thou in me, that they may become perfectly one, so that the world may know that thou hast sent me and hast loved them even as thou hast loved me" (John 17:20,23, RSV).

Jesus told us that the love that the Father gave the Son is the same love he bestows on us. We are loved by God with the identical love he gave his Son. This is the basis for a healthy self-image. It is true that we have sinned; however, it is also true that we were created in the image of God, and he is always seeking to expand that image into Godlikeness.

Last night our son cried most of the night. We were continually trying to ease his pains and to make him comfortable. Why did we do this? We did it because we are his parents. He is our son, and we love him very much. Our interest was not based upon his performance; rather, it was based upon our love.

This is a picture of the way God looks at us. Although we do not always perform very well, he is interested in our welfare. He is interested because he is our Father; we are his children, and he loves us very much. We are valuable to God.

With this revelation of God, we have the basis for a healthy self-image. Let us rejoice and be happy because God cares for you and me. In the words of the psalmist, let us also say, "How excellent is thy name, O Lord."

8
Can a Person Really Forget the Past?

Philippians 3:13

Can a person really forget the past? Of course, the answer is no; it is impossible to forget the past completely. Since this is a truth of life, what did Paul mean in Philippians 3:13 when he said that he was forgetting those things which were behind? Paul said, "Brethren, I count not myself to have apprehended: but this one thing I do, forgetting those things which are behind, and reaching forth unto those things which are before, I press toward the mark for the prize of the high calling of God in Christ Jesus."

Undoubtedly an intelligent man, Paul knew that it was impossible to forget the past completely; however, he realized that a man could come to the place in life where the past did not overshadow the present. When the apostle contended that he was leaving certain experiences in the past, I believe he meant that he was not going to allow past mistakes and experiences to overshadow his present life.

Every day I am discovering that people are depressed and defeated because of their past failures and mistakes. They allow their past failures to dominate their present thinking. Because of some past failure, they have convinced themselves that they are no good and that they are incapable of doing anything worthwhile. Not only do they doubt their abilities to accomplish anything, but they also doubt their worth as human beings.

This mental attitude is prevalent even among Christians who should know better. Many persons who have been taught that God has forgiven them of all their sins in the grace of Christ refuse to forgive themselves. Their past sins and failures have become rubber balls that they constantly kick down the avenues of their minds. Anyone who lives in the past, brooding over past mistakes, will have a difficult time living in the present. If you want to be unhappy, then constantly rethink your past failures. If you want to live victoriously, leave your past failures and disappointments in the past where they belong; instead, seek God's face as you live by faith in the present. Your *attitude* toward your past failures, not the failures themselves, is the key to a happy life.

To live in the past is to have only misery in the present. The erudite apostle understood this very clearly because of his own experience. He told the Philippians that there were certain experiences that he was going to forget as he sought the will of God. He knew that this was a must if he were to live creatively for Jesus Christ.

Consider four experiences that Paul had to leave in the past. It could be that some of the things Paul had to forget are things you need to forget. Paul had to forget the stoning of Stephen, the suffering he had endured, the stubbornness of his life, and the sickness of his body.

The Stoning of Stephen

The first mistake that Paul had to forget was the stoning of Stephen. Paul never forgot, in the literal sense, the part that he had played in the death of Christ's servant Stephen. In Acts 8:1 the Scripture relates Paul's role in Stephen's death: "Saul was consenting unto his death." Stephen preached that the gospel was for all men, Gentiles as well as Jews. When Stephen took that position, he found himself at odds with men like Saul of Tarsus. We know that Paul never forgot his role in the death of Stephen because, years later, he related his part in the death as he shared his personal testimony.

In Acts 22 we have a vivid description of a Jerusalem

mob as they tried to kill Paul. In an attempt to calm the
crowd, Paul sought to address the crowd and explain his
part in the Christian movement.

In Acts 22:20 Paul said, "When the blood of thy martyr
Stephen was shed, I also was standing by, and consenting
unto his death, and kept the raiment of them that slew
him."

In Acts 26:9-10 we have Paul's speech before King
Agrippa. As he addressed Agrippa, the apostle related his
role as a persecutor of the church. He said, "I verily thought
with myself, that I ought to do many things contrary to
the name of Jesus of Nazareth. Which thing I also did in
Jerusalem: and many of the saints did I shut up in prison
. . . and when they were put to death, I gave my voice against
them."

The great missionary apostle could never forget his part
in the death of Stephen and other members of the Christian
church; yet he did not allow these past mistakes to overshadow his present life. In Christ he had found the forgiveness of all his sins—even the sin of killing Stephen. He
believed that God had forgiven and forgotten all his sins;
hence, he had the strength to put these past failures behind
him. If Paul had allowed Stephen's death to dominate his
thinking, he would have been a depressed and defeated human being. The death of Stephen was a tragic circumstance,
but the attitude of Paul was to forget the past and to seek
God's will in the present.

All of us have sinned. The past is filled with failures and
mistakes, but God does not intend for us to live in the past.
As we have asked God to forgive us of our past sins, we
must now move forward. I think that some people believe
that God wants us to continuously brood over our past sins.
Some people have the mistaken notion that God is pleased
when we punish ourselves for something that happened
years ago. On the contrary, God is not pleased when we
do this. He knows that we can neither grow spiritually nor

be victorious in our faith if we constantly lament our past sins and failures.

Dr. Maxwell Maltz, in his book *Psycho-Cybernetics,* has made an interesting observation about people who allow their past mistakes to dominate their present thinking. He said:

> Our errors, mistakes, failures, and sometimes even our humiliations, were necessary steps in the learning process. However, they were meant to be a means to an end— and not an end in themselves. When they have served their purpose, they *should be forgotten.* If we consciously dwell upon the error, or consciously feel guilty about the error, and keep berating ourselves because of it, then— unwittingly—the error or failure itself becomes the "goal" which is consciously held in imagination and memory. The unhappiest of mortals is the man who insists upon reliving the past, over and over in imagination—continually criticizing himself for past mistakes—continually condemning himself for past sins.[1]

Sins are to be confessed. When they are confessed to God, he forgives and forgets. He does not hold our past failures before our faces. Let us learn the lesson that Paul discovered two thousand years ago: Past mistakes must not be allowed to overshadow the present. As a Christian, what is your mental attitude toward your past failures and mistakes? Are you dwelling on the past, or are you seeking God's grace? Happiness and purpose are found in the latter. You must remember that God has said, "If we confess our sins, he is faithful and just to forgive us our sins . . ." (1 John 1:9).

The Suffering Endured

Another aspect of the past that Paul had to put behind him was the persecution he had endured from others. After studying the life of Paul, we realize instantly that he experienced more than his share of physical abuse. The enemies

of Christ became the enemies of Paul, and they did everything possible to take his life. Consider a few examples of
the suffering that Paul endured as a Christian.

In Acts 14:19 Luke told us of the first missionary journey
of Paul and related the following experience: "There came
thither certain Jews from Antioch and Iconium, who per-
suaded the people, and, having stoned Paul, drew him out
of the city, supposing he had been dead." Acts 16:22–24
describes an experience which occurred during the second
missionary journey: "The multitude rose up together against
them: and the magistrates rent off their clothes, and commanded to beat them. And when they had laid many stripes
upon them, they cast them into prison, charging the jailer
to keep them safely: Who, having received such a charge,
thrust them into the inner prison, and made their feet fast
in the stocks."

Paul described this experience during his last visit to Jerusalem in Acts 21:30–32: "All the city was moved, and the
people ran together: and they took Paul, and drew him out
of the temple: and forthwith the doors were shut. And as
they went about to kill him, tidings came unto the chief
captain of the band, that all Jerusalem was in an uproar.
Who immediately took soldiers and centurions, and ran
down unto them: and when they saw the chief captain and
the soldiers, they left beating of Paul."

The references to Paul's suffering are numerous. It was
almost impossible for Paul to walk across the street without
getting a black eye; however, Paul never allowed these mis-
fortunes to dominate his thinking. He never allowed his
enemies to control his thought-life. He did not brood over
evildoers. When Paul told the Philippians that he was forgetting certain experiences, I believe that he included these
periods of tribulation. He never allowed the difficult circumstances of the past to dominate his present attitude. If he
had, he would have been discouraged and defeated. He forgave those who had hurt him in the past as his Lord had

taught him to do, and he sought God's face in the present.

What is your attitude toward those who have hurt you in the past? Do you hold a grudge? Are you still nursing old wounds? Does the remembrance of a certain person who wronged you still cause your blood to boil? If that is your mental attitude, you are a person who is having a difficult time in the present. As long as you nurse old grievances, you will be depressed and defeated. God's power cannot work in your life. I challenge you to adopt the attitude of Paul. Put those unpleasant experiences and persons behind you. Forgive them, as God has forgiven you, and live in the present. Do not allow past insults to overshadow your present life; life is too short, and there is much to be done in the Lord's work.

The Stubbornness of Paul

Another mistake that Paul had to forget was his conflict with Barnabas concerning the usefulness of John Mark. In Acts 15:36-40 the Bible states: "Some days after Paul said unto Barnabas, Let us go again and visit our brethren in every city where we have preached the word of the Lord, and see how they do. And Barnabas determined to take John, whose surname was Mark. But Paul thought not good to take him with them, who departed from them from Pamphylia, and went not with them to the work. And the contention was so sharp between them, that they departed asunder one from the other: and so Barnabas took Mark, and sailed into Cyprus; and Paul chose Silas, and departed, being recommended by the brethren unto the grace of God."

Exactly why John Mark had left them on the previous missionary journey is not known. Because of Mark's previous departure, Paul did not believe he was worthy to go on the second journey; but Barnabas was of a different mind. He wanted to give John Mark a second chance, which was characteristic of the nature of Barnabas. He was always willing to defend the weak and to give them moral support.

We know that when others refused to accept Paul into the church after his conversion, it was Barnabas who defended Paul and stood up for him before the church. It was the nature of Barnabas to be understanding and compassionate toward the underdogs. True to his forgiving spirit, Barnabas defended John Mark.

Eventually, Paul had a change of heart toward John Mark. In 2 Timothy 4:11, the apostle wrote: "Take Mark, and bring him with thee: for he is profitable to me for the ministry." In his early years Paul seemingly was a very stubborn, strong-willed individual. He and Barnabas had been very close, but the weakness of John Mark came between them. It is obvious from the tone of Acts 15 that Paul and Barnabas had a bitter argument about the usefulness of John Mark. As time passed, Paul mellowed and became more understanding toward the weaker brother. By the time Paul wrote 2 Timothy, John Mark had found a useful place alongside the elder apostle. I am sure that Paul never forgot the argument that sent him and Barnabas their separate ways. Each man had a right to his opinion, but the Lord never intended for the difference to be expressed in contention and animosity.

Paul had made a mistake. The only way to deal with a mistake is to forget it and to learn from the experience. After having learned from the experience, we need to seek God's face and grow in his grace. Dr. Maltz put it this way:

> Continually criticizing yourself for past mistakes and errors does not help matters, but on the other hand tends to perpetuate the very behavior you would change. Memories of past failures can adversely affect present performance, if we dwell upon the past mistakes and foolishly conclude—"I failed yesterday—therefore it follows that I will fail again today." If we are victimized, it is by our conscious, thinking mind and not by the "unconscious." For it is with the thinking part of our personality that

we draw conclusions, and select the "goal images" that we shall concentrate upon. The minute that we *change our minds,* and stop giving power to the past, the past with its mistakes loses its power over us.[2]

All of us have made mistakes in our relationships with others, but it does no good to brood over the past. Those who brood over their past failures are going to be depressed and defeated. What is your attitude toward your past mistakes? Why not take the attitude of the apostle Paul! Do not let the past overshadow the present; put your past mistakes behind you and seek God's grace. The Lord is always ready to mold you into his character. This is the way to victorious living.

The Sickness

Some of you may not realize it, but the apostle Paul was a very sick man. Probably his sickness was in some way related to his eyes because he said in Galatians 4:14–15, "My temptation which was in my flesh ye despised not, nor rejected; but received me as an angel of God, even as Christ Jesus. Where is then the blessedness ye spake of? for I bear you record, that, if it had been possible, ye would have plucked out your own eyes, and have given them to me."

Paul was sick, but he refused to allow the sickness to dominate his life. Without a doubt, the apostle understood the meaning of pain; however, he knew that God's grace was at work in his life to demonstrate that God's power was stronger than pain. Paul wrote in 2 Corinthians 12:7–10: "Lest I should be exalted above measure through the abundance of the revelations, there was given to me a thorn in the flesh, the messenger of Satan to buffet me, lest I should be exalted above measure. For this thing I besought the Lord thrice, that it might depart from me. And he said unto me, My grace is sufficient for thee: for my strength is made perfect in weakness. Most gladly therefore will I rather glory in my infirmities, that the power of Christ may rest upon me."

The apostle refused to allow the past to overshadow the present. He was convinced that God's grace was more than equal to all his problems.

What is your attitude toward your past failures, mistakes, and disappointments? Are you allowing the past to control the present? If that is your attitude, your life will always be lived in the realm of unhappiness and defeat. Instead, choose to follow the advice of Paul: "Forgetting those things which are behind, and reaching forth unto those things which are before."

Once a boy stood on a bridge watching the water currents go flowing by. Occasionally a piece of wood or debris would flow under the bridge and disappear from view. No matter what appeared on the surface of the water, the water slipped by as it has been doing for thousands of years. As the boy contemplated the scene, a thought came into his mind. One day everything in life would pass under the bridge. The experience of that day was never forgotten. As the boy became a man, he learned to treat his mistakes and failures as "water under the bridge."

May we never forget that one mistake or a dozen mistakes never constitute a reason to give up on life. God does not want us to quit. If we turn our past sins and failures over to him, we can live in the present.

9

Have You Ever Failed?

John 21:15–17

Have you ever failed? Of course, the answer is obvious; all of us have known failure. To live is to fail. As I counsel with people on a daily basis, I realize that failure is a stumbling block on the highway to purposeful living. Some folks have failed, and they have never been able to forget that cxpcricncc. For various reasons, they have not been able to put that experience behind them. Unwilling or unable to leave the failure in the past, these folks have walked aimlessly in the night. What is your attitude toward your past failure?

Wesley H. Hager, in his book *Conquering,* has said:

> We have not become mature Christians nor have we mastered the art of living until we learn how to handle failure. Defeat is a common experience. No one is always successful . . . . Failure is a part of life and it must be recognized and conquered before we can conquer the greater failures of our society.[1]

Today you may be drowning in the memory of past failures. Possibly your failure is in the area of marriage or children. It could be that you have failed in your occupation or in schoolwork. Whatever failure weighs heavily upon your heart, consider the message that I share with you.

I believe that we can leave our failures in the past. If you are to mature and find happiness in life, you must not allow past failures to rule your present life. The apostle Paul said that he was "forgetting those things which are behind" (Phil. 3:13). Paul had some failures in his past that he had to lay to rest. His common sense told him that if he were to mature as a Christian, he must not allow past failures to dominate his present thinking. The apostle took a new attitude toward the past, and it helped him in his Christian growth.

If you are constantly reflecting on your past failure, it is obvious that you are swimming in the muddy water of self-pity, and self-pity is the hallmark of despair and misery. Let us take a new attitude toward the past. With the help of God, may we view our past failures not as chains, but as stepping-stones to a better and more fruitful life. You cannot always change the past, but you can lay it to rest; and your *attitude* determines whether or not you do.

The life of the apostle Peter is a good example of a man's putting his past failures to rest. He serves as an inspiration to all of us who desperately want to deal positively with our failures. As we study this man's life and identify with his experiences, I call to your attention three truths about his life: the failure of Peter, the forgiveness of Peter, and the fullness of Peter.

The Failure of Peter

What do you think of when you think of the apostle Peter? I usually have a mental picture of Peter as he was preaching his great sermon at Pentecost when three thousand people were saved. This is probably the preacher instinct in me, identifying with the great revival. In Peter I see a great success; however, this is a very limited picture of the apostle. If we make a careful investigation of the gospel record, we discover that Peter had his share of failures.

The Bible tells us that Peter failed to understand and accept the purpose of God. The Bible states, "From that time on Jesus began to explain to his disciples that he must go to Jerusalem and suffer many things at the hands of the elders, chief priests and teachers of the law, and that he must be killed and on the third day be raised to life. Peter took him aside and began to rebuke him. 'Perish the thought, Lord!' he said. 'This shall never happen to you!'

"Jesus turned and said to Peter, 'Out of my sight, Satan! You are a stumbling block to me; you do not have in mind the things of God, but the things of men' " (Matt. 16:21–23, NIV).

Peter feared the words "he must be killed." With a quick response, he challenged the statement of Jesus. It could be that Peter responded in such a fashion because of his devotion to Jesus. Christ was the dearest friend he had ever known, and the prospect of seeing his friend murdered was not pleasant. It is also possible that there was a selfish motive in this response. Peter understood that if Jesus were condemned to die, he too might be placed upon a Roman cross.

Jesus heard in the voice of Peter the sinister words of Satan. Satan had a new mouthpiece as he attempted to get Jesus to disobey the will of God. We are not surprised that Jesus said, "Out of my sight, Satan." Peter had failed.

Peter failed to understand the true nature of forgiveness. The Bible reveals this experience in the life of Peter. "Peter came to Jesus and asked, 'Lord, how many times shall I forgive my brother when he sins against me? Up to seven times?'

"Jesus answered, 'I tell you, not seven times, but seventy-seven times' " (Matt. 18:21–22, NIV).

Peter must have been very proud when he said that he was willing to forgive a man at least seven times. The apostle had been taught by the rabbis that one need forgive another only three times. Peter was ready to exceed the teaching of the esteemed rabbis. The air was taken out of Peter's inflated ego when he heard Jesus say, "seventy-seven times." Forgiveness has no limits.

Peter failed to recognize his own weakness. The Bible states, "Then Jesus told them, 'This very night you will all fall away on account of me . . . . But after I have risen, I will go ahead of you into Galilee.'

"Peter replied, 'Even if all fall away on account of you, I never will.'

" 'I tell you the truth,' Jesus answered, 'this very night, before the rooster crows, you will disown me three times.'

"But Peter declared, 'Even if I have to die with you, I will never disown you' " (Matt. 26:31–35, NIV).

Perhaps Peter was convinced of his own courage. He assured Jesus that he would stand with him in the hour of need. It is possible that Peter sensed the fear in his own heart; thus, in an attempt to cover his fear before the other disciples, he made boastful claims. Whatever the thinking was in the mind of this man, he had failed to see his own weakness.

The apostle failed in prayer. The gospel record says, "He took Peter and the two sons of Zebedee along with him, and he began to be sorrowful and troubled. Then he said to them, 'My soul is overwhelmed with sorrow to the point of death. Stay here and keep watch with me.'

"Going a little farther, he fell with his face to the ground and prayed, 'My Father, if it be possible, may this cup be taken from me. Yet not as I will, but as you will.'

"Then he returned to his disciples and found them sleeping. 'Could you men not keep watch with me for one hour?' he asked Peter. 'Watch and pray so that you will not fall into temptation. The spirit is willing, but the body is weak.'

"He went away a second time and prayed, 'My Father, if it is not possible for this cup to be taken away unless I drink it, may your will be done.'

"When he came back, he again found them sleeping, because their eyes were heavy. So he left them . . . . Then he returned to the disciples and said to them, 'Are you still sleeping and resting?' " (Matt. 26:37–45, NIV).

For Jesus this hour was the most difficult in his ministry. He knew that he needed the strength of the Almighty if he were to follow completely the will of God. As he approached this moment, he asked for the companionship of Peter, James, and John. He wanted them to pray for divine guidance. Unable to sense the uniqueness of the moment or the importance of prayer, the disciples grew weary and fell asleep. He reproached Peter and said, "Could you men not keep watch with me for one hour?" For a few moments Peter stirred from his slumber, but soon he was asleep again. Peter had failed in prayer.

Peter failed in his witness. The Bible states, "Now Peter was sitting out in the courtyard, and a servant girl came to him. 'You also were with Jesus of Galilee,' she said.

"But he denied it before them all. 'I don't know what you're talking about,' he said.

"Then he went out to the gateway, where another girl saw him and said to the people there, 'This fellow was with Jesus of Nazareth.'

"He denied it again, with an oath: 'I don't know the man!'

"After a little while, those standing there went up to Peter and said, 'Surely you are one of them, for your accent gives you away.'

"Then he began to call down curses on himself and he swore to them, 'I don't know the man!' Immediately a rooster crowed. Then Peter remembered the word Jesus had spoken: 'Before the rooster crows, you will disown me three times.' And he went outside and wept bitterly" (Matt. 27:69–75, NIV).

Many thoughts must have been running through Peter's mind. After having been awakened from a deep sleep, he discovered that Jesus had been arrested by the religious authorities. Even more startling was the unwillingness of Jesus to resist the arrest. For some strange reason unknown to Peter, Jesus refused to exercise his divine power; instead, he submitted to the authorities.

After having followed Jesus to the home of the high priest, Peter was confronted with his role as a follower of Jesus.

Peter denied that he knew Jesus; and then with a heart engulfed in confusion, anxiety, and fear, Peter remembered the words of Jesus and wept. Added to his sense of confusion and fear, the burden of guilt was heavy. Peter had failed.

All of us can identify with these experiences of Peter. Like him, we have failed to obey the will of God, even when it was clearly understood. We have been bitter and angry and have withheld our forgiveness. We have been known more for our resentment than for our love. How many times have we neglected to pray? Unfortunately, prayer has been a tool that we have resorted to when all else has failed. Like the apostle, we grow weary and fall asleep. Many times God has given us the opportunity to witness, but we have hidden behind a blanket of sophistication and piety. We have been more embarrassed by our faith than challenged by it. Yes, like Peter, we know what it means to fail.

The Forgiveness of Peter

Peter failed, but how thankful we are that we do not have to leave him defeated by his failure. Many times we can learn only as we fail; often we must fail *before* we can succeed. Could it be that God allows us to fail in order to demonstrate how weak we are without his presence? Is failure God's way of deflating our egos and bringing us to faith and total submission to his will? Someone has said, "We learn by doing." Yes, failure has a way of being a stepping-stone to victory, if we turn our failures over to God.

When we fail spiritually, God does not expect us to live forever in the house called regret. When our failures are in the spiritual realm, we are to confess our failures to God and receive his forgiveness. Having received his forgiveness, we are to leave our failures in the past and not allow them to reign over our present lives.

In the Gospel of John we read, "When they had finished eating, Jesus said to Simon Peter, 'Simon son of John, do you truly love me more than these?'

" 'Yes, Lord,' he said, 'you know that I love you.'

"Jesus said, 'Feed my lambs.' Again Jesus said, 'Simon son of John, do you truly love me?'

"He answered, 'Yes, Lord, you know that I love you.'

"Jesus said, 'Take care of my sheep.' The third time he said to him, 'Simon son of John, do you love me?'

"Peter was hurt because Jesus asked him the third time, 'Do you love me?' He said, 'Lord, you know all things; you know that I love you.'

"Jesus said, 'Feed my sheep' " (John 21:15–17, NIV).

Peter and the other disciples were ready to give up. Having failed so miserably, they were ready to go back to the old fishing trade. The apostle John put it this way: "I'm going out to fish,' Simon Peter told them, and they said, 'We'll go with you.' So they went out and got into the boat, but that night they caught nothing" (John 21:3, NIV). As they threw in the towel and reverted to the fishing trade, they discovered that they were failures also as fishermen.

Jesus appeared early in the morning and told them to cast their nets on the other side of the boat. To their surprise, their nets were filled with fish. In this dramatic way, Jesus reminded them that they were still in the business of fishing for men. Christ called them back to their original task.

Peter must have been a dejected sight. As Jesus asked for Peter's love and told him to demonstrate that love by caring for people, the apostle must have remembered how he had said that he would never deny the Lord. However, in this experience, Jesus was telling Peter to forget his past failures and to go back to the business of helping other men.

The Fullness of Peter

The Bible shows us that Peter, with the help of God, was able to put his past behind him. He came to the place in life where his past failures did not overrule his present life. During the Jewish feast of Pentecost, the apostles experi-

enced the filling of the Holy Spirit. They completely opened
their lives to God, and God did a marvelous work. Concerning the role of Peter in this experience, the Bible states:
"Then Peter stood up with the Eleven, raised his voice and
addressed the crowd . . . . 'Repent and be baptized, every
one of you, in the name of Jesus Christ so that your sins
may be forgiven. And you will receive the gift of the Holy
Spirit . . . . Those who accepted this message were baptized,
and about three thousand were added to their number that
day" (Acts 2:14,38,41, NIV).

If Peter had constantly condemned himself for his past
failures, he would never have known the joy of the first
Christian revival. Peter understood that he was to turn his
failures over to God and receive the forgiveness of God.
Standing in the grace of Jesus Christ, he went out to begin
again.

In Acts 3 the writer shares with us this experience: "Now
a man crippled from birth was being carried to the temple
gate called Beautiful, where he was put every day to beg
from those going into the temple courts . . . . Then Peter
said, 'Look at us!' So the man gave them his attention, ex-
pecting to get something from them. Then Peter said, 'I
have no silver or gold, but what I have I give you. In the
name of Jesus Christ of Nazareth, walk.' . . . He jumped
to his feet and began to walk" (Acts 3:2–8, NIV). Peter was
learning to leave his failures in the past. Because of this
attitude, many people were becoming beneficiaries of a positive apostle.

Because of the healing of the cripple, Peter was brought
before the religious authorities. These were the same men
who had crucified Jesus. In a similar situation, Peter had
denied any association with Jesus; however, on this occasion
he said, "It is by the name of Jesus Christ of Nazareth,
whom you crucified but whom God raised from the dead,
that this man stands before you completely healed. When
they saw the courage of Peter and John and realized that

they were unschooled, ordinary men, they were astonished and they took note that these men had been with Jesus" (Acts 4:10,13, NIV).

Peter's influence upon the city of Jerusalem was tremendous. As he yielded his life to God, the Almighty used him to bring many people to Christ. Eventually he was arrested and beaten. The Bible relates that experience in the following way: "They arrested the apostles and put them in the public jail. Peter and the other apostles replied: 'We must obey God rather than men!' They called the apostles in and had them flogged. Then they ordered them not to speak in the name of Jesus, and let them go. The apostles left the Sanhedrin, rejoicing because they had been counted worthy of suffering disgrace for the Name" (Acts 5:18,29,40–41, NIV).

The above Scripture passages simply demonstrate that Peter was able to put his past failures into the depths of the Galilee Lake. This is not to say that Peter never failed after the Pentecost revival. Like any other man, he had his share of failures. However, he was willing to turn those failures over to God; and with the help of God, he moved ahead. He no longer allowed the past to overrule the present.

Let me challenge you to leave your failures in the past. No good can come from constantly condemning yourself for every mistake you have ever made. Turn every failure over to God and begin again in his grace. Wesley H. Hager has said:

> If we could truly know each other and understand the hearts of our fellow men, there is no doubt that our spirits would be lifted by a chorus of many voices, saying, "Lift up your hearts!" We also have known failure . . . . One of the keys to the mastery of life and the conquest of our failure is to learn with Paul that "In every thing God works for good."[2]

All I can add to that is "Amen."

10
A Second Chance

John 8:1–11

The Gospel of John states that "Jesus went to the Mount of Olives. At dawn he appeared again in the temple court, where all the people gathered around him, and he sat down to teach them. The teachers of the law and the Pharisees brought in a woman caught in adultery. They made her stand before the group and said to Jesus, 'Teacher, this woman was caught in the act of adultery. In the Law Moses commanded us to stone such women. Now what do you say?' They were using this question as a trap, in order to have a basis for accusing him.

"But Jesus bent down and started to write on the ground with his finger. When they kept on questioning him, he straightened up and said to them, 'If any one of you is without sin, let him begin stoning her.' Again he stooped down and wrote on the ground.

"At this, those who heard began to go away one at a time, the older ones first, until only Jesus was left, with the woman still standing there. Jesus straightened up and asked her, 'Woman, where are they? Has no one condemned you?'

" 'No one, sir,' she said.

" 'Then neither do I condemn you,' Jesus declared. 'Go now and leave your life of sin' " (John 8:1–11, NIV).

A minister married a lovely young couple who gave every evidence of being very much in love. About two weeks after the wedding ceremony, the bride told the minister that she wanted a divorce. The minister looked at her and said, "I do not understand. You have only been married for two weeks. Don't you remember that I said you were to be married for better or for worse?"

The young bride looked intently at the minister and said, "He is worser than I thought."

A person does not have to live very long to realize that we are "worser" than we had thought. Man is an imperfect creature. There have been times in history when men have dreamed of a time when man would be perfect in all his ways; however, world wars, the disintegration of the family, and the present lawlessness have dispelled that dream. The words of Isaiah are a constant reminder of man's nature: "All we like sheep have gone astray; we have turned every one to his own way" (Isa. 53:6).

It is the proclamation of the Bible that although a man is imperfect, he is still loved by God. The failures of man have not caused God to turn his back. Jesus knew that men were imperfect, and it was these imperfect men for whom he gave his life. Jesus has always known the tremendous potential that exists in every life, and he came to give strength to that potential. He came to people who knew a lot about failure and told them that they could begin again; he still does this today. Jesus realizes better than anyone else that all men have failed, but he knows that this does not mean that men are failures.

In John 8 we have the story of a woman who had failed. Through her encounter with Jesus she discovered that although she had failed, she was not a failure. She was offered a second chance. As we look at this Scripture lesson, consider three ideas: the accusers, the accused, and the advocate.

The Accusers

The accusers of this woman were the Pharisees and the teachers of the law, folks who never missed church. This was the crowd that worshiped, prayed, and tithed on a weekly basis—the good folks.

Have you ever noticed that sometimes the most critical people in the world are the people who go to church? Have you ever noticed in your own life that there are times when you do more accusing than anyone else? I have asked these questions of myself on more than one occasion. I have concluded that often I am quick to point the accusing finger in the hope that it will cover my own failings. As long as we are focusing on the sins of others, we are not compelled to view our own sins. By making the other man's sins large, we hope to make our own sins small.

If everyone knew about our secret sins, I do not believe that we would be so outspoken concerning the sins of others. Could it be that when others fail, we are reminded of our own failures? Rather than looking honestly at our failings, we tend to magnify the sins of others in the hope that our own haunting thoughts will be drowned in the sea of accusation. Confession can be painful, and no one likes to experience pain; thus, the easy way out is to shout from the rooftops the sins of others.

The timing of this episode was perfect. The accusers waited until a large crowd had gathered, and then they brought forth this rag doll and hurled her at the feet of Jesus. She was like a toy in the hands of destructive children. These churchgoers were not really concerned about this woman's life-style. They simply wanted a means of embarrassing Jesus before the public.

As the woman stood defenseless before the crowd, the Pharisees shouted: "Teacher, this woman was caught in the act of adultery. In the Law Moses commanded us to stone such women. Now what do you say?"

Theoretically, the Pharisees were correct in saying that the law decreed death for anyone caught committing adultery. According to Leviticus 20:10, "The man that committeth adultery with another man's wife, even he that committeth adultery with his neighbor's wife, the adulterer and the adulteress shall surely be put to death." Deuteronomy

22:22 puts it this way: "If a man be found lying with a woman married to an husband, then they shall both of them die, both the man that lay with the woman, and the woman."

Notice carefully that the Scripture says that both the man and the woman were to be put to death; but in our Scripture passage, no mention is made of the man. Where was the adulterer? Why did the Pharisees exclude him? If they were truly concerned about the law, why did they bring only one guilty party?

The women's liberation movement has said some things that all of us need to hear. They have reminded us, and rightly so, that we have a double standard in regard to the sexes.

A man can commit adultery and be unfaithful to his family and very little is said about it. In fact, if a young man commits fornication, usually it is said that he is "sowing his wild oats" as he becomes a man. However, if a young girl fails in her sexual conduct, she is looked upon as disgraced; and her plight becomes a juicy piece of news for every malicious tongue in the community. We have a double standard now just as they had a double standard during the time of Christ.

Of course, we realize that these ministers were not truly concerned about the law of this woman's conduct. If Jesus agreed that she should be stoned, then they could say to the people that he was not a man of compassion and mercy. If he disapproved of the stoning, they could accuse him of breaking the law. No matter which position he took, the teachers of the law were confident that they could end the ministry of Jesus in a very dramatic way.

The Accused

Who was this woman who stood before Jesus on that morning in Jerusalem? Was she an unfaithful wife? Was she a woman who had become disenchanted with life and had decided to throw all reason to the wind? Was she the product of a broken home, one who had, out of desperation, sought the arms of an understanding lover? History does not record her name, and this is probably best; all we know for sure is that she had failed and that her failure had become a test case for all humanity to view.

She was not the first woman to have the accusing finger pointed in her direction. As I have read of this experience, I have come to see one of the most tragic experiences in all of the Bible. I have tried to imagine the fear that must have gripped her mind as she heard the words of death pronounced in her ears. I have tried to picture her facial expression, which was probably twisted and distorted by guilt, shame, and embarrassment. In my mind I have looked into her eyes and seen both horror and hope as she waited for Jesus to speak. Most of all, I have visualized a person who had failed and who had been informed by the religious community that there was no room in this world for failures.

As I read this experience, I was reminded of Nathaniel Hawthorne's *The Scarlet Letter*. In the novel a Puritan minister, Arthur Dimmesdale, has an affair with a lady of his church, Hester Prynne. Hester gives birth to his child, but she refuses to tell the community the name of the father. Dimmesdale does not have the courage to tell his parishioners that he has failed. He allows Hester to face the angry community alone. For punishment, it was decreed that Hester must wear a large letter *A* on her bosom and stand three hours every day on the platform in the center of town. Hawthorne described it this way:

> When the young woman—the mother of this child—stood fully revealed before the crowd, it seemed to be her first impulse to clasp the infant closely to her bosom. . . . In a moment, however, wisely judging that one token of her shame would but poorly serve to hide another, she took the baby in her arms, and, with a burning blush, and yet a haughty smile . . . looked around at her townspeople

and neighbors. On the breast of her gown, in fine red cloth, surrounded with an elaborate embroidery and fantastic flourishes of gold thread, appeared the letter *A* . . . . Could it be true? She clutched the child so fiercely to her breast, that it sent forth a cry; she turned her eyes downward at the scarlet letter, and even touched it with her finger, to assure herself that the infant and the shame were real. Yes!—These were her realities,—all else had vanished.[1]

Like Hester Prynne, the woman of John 8 stood exposed to the world's gaze. She was helpless and hopeless, and what she desperately needed was a good lawyer.

The Advocate

As I look at this dear woman's plight, I am reminded of the words of John: "My dear children, I write this to you so that you will not sin. But if anybody does sin, we have one who speaks to the Father in our defense—Jesus Christ, the Righteous One. He is the atoning sacrifice for our sins, and not only for ours but also for the sins of the whole world" (1 John 2:1–2, NIV).

This lady needed a good lawyer; and although she did not realize it immediately, she had the best lawyer who ever lived—Jesus Christ. He speaks to the Father on our behalf.

Christ came to identify with failures. He came to people like you and me to declare that God loves us, even when we fail. We need to remember that no matter how many times we have failed, no matter what that failure may be, and regardless of what society may say about our failures, Jesus Christ stands ready to defend us before the judgment bar of man and God.

As the Pharisees taunted Jesus and ridiculed the woman, Jesus stooped down and wrote on the ground. There is no record of what he wrote, and we can only speculate at this point. Barclay tells us in his commentary that the normal Greek word for *write* is *graphein;* however, the word used here is *katagraphein*. This word means to write down a record against someone. Barclay suggests that it is possible that Jesus was writing a list of the Pharisees' sins as they denounced the woman for adultery.[2]

Personally, I believe that Jesus was embarrassed by the episode. His heart must have ached as he saw men who should have known better acting like tyrants. The Pharisees were the keepers of the law; thus, they should have been the first to teach that God's grace is the answer to man's sin.

When people have failed, they usually are well aware of their failure. It is true that some people act as if sin really does not cause guilt and shame; however, most of the time these folks are only putting up a good front. When men fail, they do not need a pointing finger of accusation; on the contrary, they need the open hand of God's grace.

Jesus always knew how to break up a crowd. With devastating force, he said: "If anyone of you is without sin, let him begin stoning her." A more literal translation would be, "If you have never had an evil thought, kill her."

It is true that the woman had failed, but Jesus demonstrated that the Pharisees had also failed. When faced with their own sins, they could do no more than drop the stones and walk away. Jesus then turned to the woman and said: "Woman, where are they? Has no one condemned you?"

"No one, sir," she said.

"Then neither do I condemn you," Jesus declared. "Go now and leave your life of sin."

Jesus was not condoning what the woman had done. Jesus always spoke against sin and constantly urged people to repent; however, he always offered grace in exchange of guilt. I believe that this was what he was offering to this woman. Seemingly she too came to see that she could exchange her guilt for God's grace.

We are *saved* by grace. Ephesians 2:8 makes this clear: "It is by grace you have been saved, through faith—and this not from yourselves, it is the gift of God" (NIV). Furthermore, we must also realize that we are *sustained* by grace. Every Christian has failed and can be certain that he will fail again, but there is hope for every failure. The God who has saved us by his grace is the same God who continues to forgive us through his grace. Every time a Christian fails, God says: "Give me that failure, and I will give you my grace." Jesus said to the woman in our Scripture passage, "Give me your failure, and I will give you my grace."

Jesus told this woman to go and sin no more. I take that command in two ways. First, he told her to leave the failure in the past; she was not to condemn herself continuously for her past sin. Jesus knew that if this woman lived the rest of her days looking over her shoulder, she would never have a purposeful life. Second, she was not to go back to her old life of sin; the recognition of God's grace was her invitation to choose a new and different life-style. She was given a second chance.

The Master says the same thing to us when we fail. We must see that in God's eyes there is no such thing as a failure; people fail, but they are not failures. With God's help, we must turn our failures over to God; and he, in turn, will give us his grace. I believe that this is a fair exchange. God does not point the accusing finger; instead, he offers his hand and says, "Take my grace."

11

Restoration of a Failure

Mark 5:1–10

For the past eight months, residents of central Florida reported that there was a "wild" man living in the swamps. At first authorities thought that the people had allowed their imaginations to run rampant. Because of the mosquitoes, cottonmouths, rattlesnakes, and alligators, it was believed that even if a man had entered the swamp, he would last only a few days. Nevertheless, there actually was a "wild" man in the swamps because he was eventually spotted by a policeman; and as incredible as it seems, he had somehow survived the swamp environment for several months.

The "wild" man was a Taiwanese merchant seaman named Hu Tu-mei. Fearing that he would be sent back to Taiwan because of his bizarre behavior, he had escaped from a Tampa hospital into the swamp. Occasionally he broke into trailers to steal food, but most of the time he ate whatever he found in the swamp. His diet had consisted of snakes, turtles, and armadillos. At one abandoned campsite, it was discovered that he had killed a four-foot alligator and had eaten the tail and feet.

When the authorities captured him, he said that he had fled into the swamps because he knew that he would be executed if he were returned to Taiwan. His body was completely covered with insect bites; but, amazingly, he was in good condition.

On the fourth day after his capture, a police officer discovered that Hu Tu-mei had committed suicide by hanging himself. The authorities had really wanted to help, but no one had been able to unravel the mystery of the terror that possessed his mind. This man knew the meaning of failure; the real tragedy is that he was never able to overcome it.

When I read of that experience, it reminded me of a similar experience in the Bible. Mark 5:1–20 states: "They went across the lake to the region of the Gerasenes. When Jesus got out of the boat, a man with an evil spirit came from the tombs to meet him. This man lived in the tombs, and no one could bind him any more, not even with a chain. For he had often been chained hand and foot, but he tore the chains apart and broke the irons on his feet. No one was strong enough to subdue him. Night and day among the tombs and in the hills he would cry out and cut himself with stones.

"When he saw Jesus from a distance, he ran and fell on his knees in front of him. He shouted at the top of his voice, 'What do you want with me, Jesus, Son of the Most High God? Swear to God that you won't torture me!' For Jesus was saying to him, 'Come out of this man, you evil spirit!'

"Then Jesus asked him, 'What is your name?'

" 'My name is Legion,' he replied, 'for we are many.' And he begged Jesus again and again not to send them out of the area.

"A large herd of pigs was feeding on the nearby hillside. The demons begged Jesus, 'Send us among the pigs; allow us to go into them.' He gave them permission, and the evil spirits came out and went into the pigs. The herd, about two thousand in number, rushed down the steep bank into the lake and were drowned.

"Those tending the pigs ran off and reported this in the town and countryside, and the people went out to see what had happened. When they came to Jesus, they saw the man who had been possessed by the legion of demons, sitting there, dressed and in his right mind; and they were afraid.

Those who had seen it told the people what had happened to the demon-possessed man—and told about the pigs as well. Then the people began to plead with Jesus to leave their region.

"As Jesus was getting into the boat, the man who had been demon-possessed begged to go with him. Jesus did not let him, but said, 'Go home to your family and tell them how much the Lord has done for you, and how he has had mercy on you.' So the man went away and began to tell in the Decapolis how much Jesus had done for him. And all the people were amazed" (NIV).

In this Scripture passage, please consider three facts: the description of the demon-possessed, the deliverance of the demon-possessed, and the desire of the demon-possessed.

The Description

After calming the storm on the lake, Jesus was confronted with the raging storm of a twisted mind. Jesus was in the region of Gerasene or Gadarene, Gentile country that lay on the east side of the lake of Galilee. Jesus probably made his way to this area to get away from the crowds so that he could rest. During the journey, he had demonstrated his power over nature and had called his apostles to live by faith.

Once on the other side of the lake, he was confronted by a man who had an evil spirit. Because of his strange behavior, this man lived in the tombs—caves that had been hewed out of the mountains for burial purposes. He had unusual strength and could break the chains of those who tried to bind him.

Because of his behavior, we can well understand why the community would be frightened and would desire to have him chained and locked away; but chains were of no use, and he roamed the hills night and day crying out to the whole world. In his sickness, he took rocks and slashed his own body; truly he must have been a frightening and pathetic sight. To the community he was a failure; and in his rational moments, he too must have dwelled on his own failure. However, to Jesus he was a person, loved by God, with unlimited potential for good. Jesus saw in him a man who could put his failures in the past and begin again.

How are we to understand this man's condition? Was he demon-possessed in the literal sense? Was his body indwelt by "evil spirits" or "fallen angels"? Should we view this man as a mentally ill person? If this man had lived today, would he have been classified as schizophrenic? There are many different opinions concerning these questions.

The theme of demon possession has become very popular. Far too many people have carried this idea to the extreme; some folks are seeing demons behind every tree. Jack Taylor, a well-known Southern Baptist pastor, wrote a book on demons entitled *Victory Over the Devil,* a book that did much to popularize the demon idea among Southern Baptists. In his latest book, *After the Spirit Comes,* Taylor said:

> Few people ever plunge into a study of the devil and demons without getting imbalanced at least temporarily. There is something about this area of truth that is particularly appealing to the human mind. I did not escape this pitfall . . . . While some "go to seed" over finding demons under every chair and behind every frown, others with equally expensive error totally deny their existence and thus preclude the possibility of deliverance. I plead for balance.[1]

Recently in England, during a religious service at a Christian church, a charismatic lady claimed to have cast forty demons out of Michael Taylor. After the service Michael Taylor went home and brutally murdered his twenty-nine-year-old wife. With his bare hands, he literally tore her face away. This experience, as well as numerous others like it, is a constant reminder that demon possession has been carried to the extreme. The vast majority of Christians have not been called of God to exorcise demons.

Professor Gary R. Collins has said that "unfortunately, there are sincere Christians who have become so concerned about demonology that they have developed fanciful theories about demons which have no basis in the scripture and which distract from the message of the Word of God."[2]

It should be noted that the ministry of Jesus was not totally given to dealing with demons, and to overstress his role in this area is to ignore the whole of the New Testament. Second, one should observe that the accounts of demon possession in the ministry of Jesus never occurred in the "heart" of Israel. When Jesus encountered demons, it was always in lands bordering the country of Israel, areas known for superstitious, paganistic ways.

If we see this experience as modern-day mental illness, we are still confronted with some very important questions. Modern psychiatry has taken a new twist in recent days in its approach to mental illness, an approach worthy of our investigation.

Traditionally, those who have been classified as mentally ill and thus placed in mental institutions have been assumed not to be responsible for their behavior. The traditional approach in psychiatry had been to blame the patient's circumstances for his abnormal behavior. Statements from a chaplain serving a state mental hospital adequately summarized this idea:

> First of all, there is little you can do as ministers for people in a mental hospital. Secondly, what you can do is support the patient's right to feel injured by others. Thirdly, it is important to understand that in a mental institution people with guilt no longer are subjected to rebuke from others outside; the pressure is off, and in this way they quietly lose their guilt and get well.

Fourthly, we must consider people in mental hospitals not as violators of conscience but as victims of their conscience. Finally, when we look at their erratic behavior, it seems to be sin, but it isn't; the patient is not really responsible for his actions. He can't help what he's doing; he's sick. Often he blames himself for what he can't help, for what isn't his fault, and this is a cause of his problems. Consequently bad behavior as blameworthy is taboo in a mental hospital. The usual religious approach of responsibility, guilt, confession and forgiveness is no good here. The patients' consciences are already too severe. These people are morally neutral persons, and all we can do is be ventilators for them.[3]

Although the above statements portray the traditional approach to mental illness, this is not the only approach. A revolution is now taking place in the fields of psychiatry and psychology. Two leading figures in this revolution are O. Hobart Mowrer and William Glasser. Mowrer, in his book *The Crisis in Psychiatry and Religion,* and Glasser, in his book *Reality Therapy,* challenge the traditional concept that a mentally ill person is not really responsible for his behavior. These men, while working in mental hospitals with mental patients, have demonstrated that many people are in mental hospitals because they have violated their consciences, not because of hormone deficiencies or damaged brain cells. The problem is sinful behavior, and it can only be corrected by the confession of sin and the assuming of personal responsibility. According to these doctors, most patients are not mentally ill; rather, they are morally ill.

Mowrer claims, because of his experience with "mentally ill" patients, that most of the time the mental patient's problems are moral rather than medical. The patient suffers from real guilt because he is a violator of his conscience, not a victim; and he can be cured only by refusing to blame others for his acts and by assuming responsibility for his own behavior. Problems are not solved by the ventilation of feelings (the traditional approach of psychiatry), but rather by the confession of sin.

Jay E. Adams, a Christian minister and seminary professor who worked with Mowrer at two mental institutions in Illinois, came to see through firsthand experience that most people were in the Kankakee and Galesburg mental institutions because of sinful behavior. He wrote that "there is a mounting conviction that much bizarre behavior must be interpreted as camouflage intended to divert attention from one's otherwise deviant behavior."[4]

In his book *Competent to Counsel,* Adams gives two typical illustrations of what he saw and experienced while working with Mowrer in the Illinois mental institutions. Steve was a young man who had been placed in an Illinois mental institution as a catatonic schizophrenic. He refused to speak and walked as if in a stupor. The counselors attacked his silence, saying that they knew he was faking. Eventually Steve began cooperating with the counselors, who soon discovered that he indeed did not have a mental disorder. Steve confessed that while at college he had refused to study and was obviously about to fail. Rather than face the music with his parents, he began acting in a bizarre fashion. When he realized that this threw his parents off the track, he decided to continue his antics. He was classified as mentally ill, but his real problem was shame, guilt, and fear. The irony of all this is that the longer he was treated as a mentally ill person, the greater was his guilt; the traditional treatment only made his situation worse. Steve was challenged to accept responsibility for his acts and to change his attitude. Although this approach was certainly not the traditional approach in psychiatry, it brought healing to Steve.

Mary is another example of moral rather than mental illness. She had been diagnosed as a manic-depressive. When a counselor approached her, she would shout and scream.

Under the therapy used by Mowrer, she was approached and told:

> O be quiet! Unless you stop this kind of nonsense and get down to business, we simply can't help you, Mary. Surely a young girl like you doesn't want to spend the rest of her life in this institution. We know that you have real problems, and we know that there is something wrong in your life. Now let's start talking turkey.[5]

Under this new therapy, Mary confessed all. Her confession was a sordid tale of sin. She was helped because the counselors refused to be shaken by her screams. Mary found help when she confessed her sins and exhibited a willingness to change her ways.

It is quite possible and probable that the demon-influenced man of Mark 5 had a moral problem that expressed itself in bizarre behavior. If this can be true today, it certainly could have been true then. The root of his problem was sin. The demons had control of his mind because he had, by an act of the will, given himself to do the devil's bidding. He was morally responsible for his condition; in no way could he "pass the buck" to the demons.

The Deliverance

When Jesus saw the demon-controlled man, he said, "Come out of this man, you evil spirit!" The construction of the Greek text indicates that Jesus repeatedly commanded the unclean spirit to come from the man. Because of the command of Jesus, this pathetic man ran toward Jesus and fell at his feet and cried, "Swear to God that you won't torture me!"

At this point in the biblical narrative, it is difficult to tell whether it is the man speaking or the demons. When Jesus asked the man his name, he or "they" responded by saying, "My name is Legion, for we are many." The term *legion* was used to refer to six thousand Roman troops. Does this mean that six thousand demons inhabited this man? No one can say conclusively, but the term probably is intended to stress the intensity of this man's sickness.

Close to where Jesus and this man stood, a herd of swine was feeding. Sensing that Jesus had power over them, the demons asked to be sent into the swine. After Jesus had given his permission, the evil spirits inhabited the pigs. At this point, the swine rushed madly down the cliff into the lake, where they drowned. How are we to understand this experience?

I believe that the demonic man needed a vivid demonstration that Christ really had the power to heal his body; therefore, Jesus gave him a visual experience with which he could identify. For those who were tending the pigs, it was a frightening experience that caused them to flee; for the demoniac, it was visual proof that Jesus had broken the rule of Satan in his life. Although Jesus had allowed the unclean spirits to flee into the pigs, he had done so not because of their request but because the demoniac needed dramatic proof that Christ had power over the demons.

When the citizens of the vicinity finally came out to see the miracle that Jesus had performed, they saw the former madman "dressed and in his right mind." Although the text does not say so, Jesus did more than simply exorcise the demons; he also invited the man to let God rule in his life.

The removal of demons is not synonymous with conversion. Jesus stressed this in his gospel preaching. In Matthew 12:43–45 he said: "When an evil spirit comes out of a man, it goes through arid places seeking rest and does not find it. Then it says, 'I will return to the house I left.' When it arrives, it finds the house unoccupied, swept clean and put in order. Then it goes and takes with it seven other spirits more wicked than itself, and they go in and live there. And the final condition of that man is worse than the first" (NIV). This healed man experienced both the healing of his body and the healing of his spirit because he was born again into the kingdom of God through a personal acceptance of the lordship of Christ.

The Desire

When the people returned to the scene of the miracle and saw what Jesus had done, they pleaded with him to leave their region. It is possible that this request was made because of fear, but fear of what? Could it be that these people feared losing more of their pigs? Perhaps the request was based upon economic implications; and if this is true, then it is obvious that they were more interested in pigs than they were in seeing a failure made new. Their desire was very simple: Do not get us involved.

The desire of the healed man, however, was very different: he wanted to be with Jesus. The Bible says that he "begged to go with him." This was the final proof that this man had truly been converted; those who have been born again want to spend their days in the presence of Christ.

Jesus would not allow the man to go with him because he had another mission for him: "Go home to your family and tell them how much the Lord has done for you, and how he has had mercy on you."

The most difficult people to witness to are the members of our own families. We would rather witness to people in Columbus or China than to witness to our next-door neighbors because our neighbors know us; the people in China do not. This man had been a complete failure, and the members of his family saw this very clearly; nevertheless, Jesus directed him back to his own community. Jesus' command was intended to show this man that failures can be healed and that he must put his failures in the past. He could not allow his past mistakes to overrule his new life; he was to forget the past and live for God in the present.

All of us have known failure. Like the demoniac's, our failures have forced us to retreat into our own little "secret caves," where we have felt unloved and worthless to ourselves and to others. This Scripture passage, however, reminds us that we are deeply loved by the Father no matter what our failures may be. The Father believes that we are valuable and that our worth cannot be measured in human terms. The Father values your worth so much that he sent his Son, Jesus Christ, to be your loving Savior and Lord. This is not the time to retreat into your secret cave and kick yourself for your past sins. Confess your sins to the Father and receive his grace and love. Now is the time to exchange failure for forgiveness.

Thomas A. Harris, in his book *I'm OK—You're OK,* has given us valuable insight into the human personality. Many of us are sick because we see ourselves as "not OK"; however, we are reminded by the ministry of Jesus that his love has the power to convince us that we are deeply loved by God. Like the demoniac, we stand before the Savior and shout with joy, "I'm really OK because of your love and grace!"

12
Yesterday Is a Closed Book

Acts 13:13

When Paul and Barnabas left Antioch to begin their first missionary journey, they took with them John Mark, the nephew of Barnabas. As far as the church at Antioch was concerned, John Mark had all the essentials necessary for making a contribution to the missionary effort. However, after they had left Cyprus and landed on the continent of Asia Minor, John Mark left Paul and Barnabas and returned home.

The Scripture does not tell us why John Mark left the missionary party. Some have suggested that he was homesick; others have concluded that he resisted Paul's leadership. When the missionaries left Antioch, Barnabas was the unmistakable leader of the group; however, by the time the missionaries reached Perga, Paul had assumed the reins of leadership. Since Barnabas was John Mark's uncle, Mark may have left the group because he was dissatisfied that his uncle was no longer in charge. A few scholars have suggested that John Mark left the party because Paul was taking the gospel to the Gentiles; perhaps his Jewish prejudice would not allow him to welcome non-Jews into the family of God. For whatever reason, Mark went home.

When Paul and Barnabas got ready to begin their second missionary journey, Barnabas wanted to give John Mark a second chance. Paul, however, would not concur with the request, and bitter words were spoken between the two missionaries. Because of the dispute over John Mark, Paul and

Barnabas parted company and went their separate ways. Because of Mark's failure on the first missionary endeavor, Paul did not believe that John Mark was capable or worthy of consideration for the second missionary outreach.

As time passed, though, Paul had a change of heart toward Mark. In fact, Paul said to Timothy, "Take Mark, and bring him with thee: for he is profitable to me for the ministry" (2 Tim. 4:11). During the years after the Paul-Barnabas-Mark missionary effort, Mark had made a definite contribution to the gospel cause; and Paul had recognized the worth and value of the young man's life. In the beginning of the gospel story, Mark had failed; nevertheless, as the church grew, Mark became a vessel of godliness which helped in the creation of God's people.

What would have happened to Mark if he had constantly relived the fact that he had failed on the first missionary journey? The answer is obvious: He would never have accomplished anything in the Lord's work. Anyone who constantly relives past failures or criticizes himself for past failures finds his present life to be sheer misery. To live successfully, we must not allow our past failures to overrule our present undertakings. John Mark was able to understand that yesterday, with all its failures, had to be a closed book.

What is failure anyway? How would you define failure? Let me share with you the Christian definition of failure:

Failure doesn't mean you are a failure . . . . *It does mean* you haven't succeeded yet.

Failure doesn't mean you have accomplished nothing . . . . *It does mean* you have learned something.

Failure doesn't mean you have been a fool . . . . *It does mean* you had a lot of faith.

Failure doesn't mean you've been disgraced . . . . *It does mean* you were willing to try.

Failure doesn't mean you don't have it . . . . *It does mean* you have to do something in a different way.

> *Failure doesn't mean* you are inferior . . . . *It does mean*
> you are not perfect.
> *Failure doesn't mean* you've wasted your life . . . . *It does*
> *mean* you have a reason to start afresh.
> *Failure doesn't mean* you'll never make it . . . . *It does*
> *mean* it will take a little longer.
> *Failure doesn't mean* God has abandoned you . . . . *It*
> *does mean* God has a better idea![1]

No man is a total failure. John Mark understood this, and you need to understand this. There is always hope for the future. During World War II a hospital in France for the mentally insane was struck by a bomb. The explosion permitted all of the 156 patients to escape. All of the patients had been placed in this hospital because they were considered to be hopeless cases. The authorities searched diligently for the patients, but it took many years to locate all of them. Eventually it was discovered that of the 156 former patients, 86 had become productive, healthy, useful persons. These men and women had refused to allow past failures to dictate their new lives; yesterday was a closed book.

Let me suggest three ways whereby we might conquer our past failures: accept the Almighty's abundant help; adopt an attitude of faith; and actively become involved in helping others.

The Almighty's Abundant Help

How do we conquer our past failures? We must have the help of God; we must always remember that he loves us. He does not view us as failures; on the contrary, he sees the unlimited potential that is present in every life. He created us for victory, not for defeat. When we fail, God is always present to give us strength to begin again.

We are very important to God. He would not have sent his Son to die for us if he had considered us unimportant. Jesus went through all the villages of Israel proclaiming the worth of man to God. It was Jesus who said, "The Spirit of the Lord is upon me, because he hath anointed me to preach the gospel to the poor; he hath sent me to heal the brokenhearted, to preach deliverance to the captives, and recovering of sight to the blind, to set at liberty them that are bruised, To preach the acceptable year of the Lord" (Luke 4:18–19). Yes, Jesus lives to give strength to those who have failed.

Across the hills of Galilee came the beggars, the blind, the sick, the cripples, the outcasts, the prostitutes, the tax collectors, the lepers, the aristocrats, the soldiers, the politicians, and the children to hear from Jesus that one specific truth: God cares. People from every phase of society discovered through the ministry of Jesus that every man, no matter what his position in society, is important to God.

Even as Christians, we fail. If our failure is the result of sin, the Bible tells us that "If we confess our sins, he is faithful and just to forgive us our sins, and to cleanse us from all unrighteousness" (1 John 1:9). Because of the forgiveness of God, we can make yesterday a closed book.

The Lord realizes far better than we do that to live in the past only brings misery. He wants us to turn those past failures over to him and to move forward in his strength because no good comes from reliving past mistakes. The apostle Paul said, "We are more than conquerors through him that loved us" (Rom. 8:37). This means that with his help we are more than conquerors over our past failures. Wesley H. Hager, in his book *Conquering,* has said:

> Life is serious and we are so made that we cannot treat failure as if it were success and success as if it were defeat. When success is ours, we are happy and grateful to God; but when we face defeat and failure, it is difficult to remember that 'in everything' God is present. Yet it is one of life's greatest lessons to learn that God in our failures is working with us to make us conquerors.[2]

The apostle Peter had his share of failures: he was limited in his forgiveness, weak in prayer, and proficient in cursing the air blue; he had a loud mouth and a weak will. However, Jesus never gave up on him. If Peter had constantly relived in his mind that time when he had denied the Lord before the campfire, he would have been a defeated Christian. Rather than doing that, though, with the help of Christ, he put that failure behind him. Yesterday at the fireside became a closed book.

The same can be said of Paul. If Paul had constantly tormented himself because of his past involvement in the stoning of Stephen, life would have been nothing more than a hollow shell. Paul realized that God did not expect or want him to criticize himself constantly for past failure. For Paul, yesterday with all its failures became a closed book because God helped him to close that book.

Recently a young girl who had been a former dope addict spoke at a Billy Graham Crusade. She told of how Christ had changed her life and of her work in helping others break the tyranny of dope. It is true that in the past she had failed miserably; but what would have happened if this young girl, after conversion, had constantly condemned herself for her past failures? Where would she be now if she had continually relived her past failures and the memories of how she had hurt so many? I will tell you where she would be—on the ash heap. However, her message does not stress the past; rather, it stresses the power of the living Christ. She tells of what Christ is doing now and will do tomorrow. She is allowing yesterday to remain a closed book.

The Attitude of Faith

A second way in which we can put our failures to rest is through the attitude of faith. History reveals numerous men and women who have conquered their past failures through the attitude of faith. If they were able to turn failures into victories, then we can do the same.

Many of us know of Dr. David Livingstone, the great missionary-doctor of Africa. A man of strong character, he gave his life for the people of Africa. With the gospel he brought healing to many souls, and with medicine he brought balm to many diseased bodies.

At one point during his travels across the dark continent, he came to the ruins of a Christian church. This church had been established by the Jesuits hundreds of years before the advent of Dr. Livingstone; but it was now in ruins, giving testimony to the failure of the Jesuits. As he looked at the scene, dark despair choked his mind. In his journal he wrote: "Why should I go on? Is it worthwhile going on trying to open up Africa with its teeming millions to the Christian gospel when tomorrow morning I, too, may be knocked on the head by ignorant savages?"

We know that Dr. Livingstone did go on. He had more than his share of failures, but he never gave in to those failures. For him, yesterday with all its failures was simply a closed book. He allowed his failures to become stepping-stones to greater accomplishments rather than barriers to his work.

I challenge you to have the same attitude toward your failures. Turn those failures over to God and move ahead with his grace. Yesterday must and can become a closed book.

In 1925 there was a young man who desperately wanted to play in the major leagues. He was a good hitter, but he had a very difficult time fielding the ball. He was extremely thin, thus giving the appearance that he might topple over at any moment. One day the great Ty Cobb saw this young man trying to play ball and sarcastically referred to him as "Piano Legs." Eventually the dream of "Piano Legs" being in the big leagues became a reality, and he soon became one of the greatest ball players of all times. Each time he was knocked down by his failures, he kept getting up to play ball. He set the record for the most consecutive games ever played—2,130. Today this man is respectfully remembered, not as "Piano Legs," but as Lou Gehrig.

Gehrig attained his goal of playing in the major leagues because he never gave in to his failures. For him, yesterday was a closed book because his attitude was to forget past failures and move ahead to victory. In his opinion, failures were simply learning experiences whereby a man could improve.

Because of an incurable disease, Lou Gehrig had to give up baseball. On July 4, 1939, Yankee stadium observed Lou Gehrig Day, on which occasion Gehrig said, "For the past two weeks you have been reading about a bad break; yet today I consider myself the luckiest man on the face of the earth."

Even after having been forced out of baseball by a strange disease, Gehrig refused to quit. He started a new career with the New York parole office, where he worked until his death in 1941. Even in sickness, this immortal of the sports world refused to swim in the polluted waters of self-pity. Yesterday was a closed book. Instead of giving in to his circumstances, he lived by an attitude of faith.

Abraham Lincoln knew the meaning of failure. He was a business failure; he nearly failed in the law profession; he was defeated in his first attempt to be elected to the Illinois state legislature; he was defeated in his first attempt to be elected to the United States Congress; he was defeated in his bid to become commissioner of the General Land Office; in 1856 he was defeated in his bid for the vice-presidency; and in 1858 he was defeated in his second attempt to be elected to Congress. However, even after all these failures, he was elected President of the United States in 1861.

Experiences in the life of Abraham Lincoln teach all of us that failure is not the end. A thousand failures is no reason to give up. Like Abe, we must not allow our past failures to overrule our present lives. Like Paul, we must forget those things which are behind and press forward.

Activity on Behalf of Others

Once a man plagued by his failures contemplated suicide.
As he sought an appropriate place to end it all, he happened
to pick up a copy of the *Saturday Evening Post*. On the
inside of the magazine, he found these words by Archibald
Rutledge:

> Oh, gallant heart defeated
> Now gazing toward the west
> Where this day's splendor crumbles
> Disastrous and unblessed.
>
> Look 'til the deathlike darkness
> By star glorified
> Until you see another dream
> Beyond that dream that died.[3]

These words banished all thoughts of suicide. The man
determined to begin anew. We conquer our failures when
we acknowledge them and then make an effort to begin
again. A new beginning is accomplished only with the help
of God and the attitude of faith.

The third way we can make yesterday a closed book is
by becoming involved in helping others. Unselfish love for
others is a tonic to the soul. At this very moment, someone
needs you to care for him. Without you, his life may be
incomplete. It could be a member of your family; possibly
it is your neighbor or the person with whom you work. You
see, you really do not have time to indulge in self-pity because of your past failures; already too many are stuck in
the mud of self-pity, and they need you to lift them out of
despair.

Zacchaeus was a man who had failed. From a material
standpoint, he was a great success. He had money, power,
position, prestige—all the outward symbols of success. However, inwardly he was a total failure because his wealth

had been acquired through fraud, deceit, cheating, and a host of other selfish devices.

One day Jesus met Zacchaeus. They dined at Zacchaeus' mansion, and the tax collector was converted. Luke said, "Zacchaeus stood up and said to the Lord, 'Look, Lord! Here and now I give half of my possessions to the poor, and if I have cheated anybody out of anything, I will pay back four times the amount.'

"Jesus said to him, 'Today salvation has come to this house, because this man, too, is a son of Abraham. For the Son of Man came to seek and to save what was lost'" (Luke 19:8–10, NIV).

Notice that Zacchaeus turned his failures over to God, and by faith he put his life into the hands of Jesus. Having made yesterday a closed book, he began helping others; he became involved in the business of restoration. Instead of condemning himself for all his failures, he gave himself in service of others.

Never give in to your failures. Instead, turn every failure over to God and receive his strength. By faith, meet today and conquer it; get involved in helping others. You will then discover that yesterday has become a closed book and that today is "the day that the Lord has made; we will rejoice and be glad in it" (Ps. 118:24).

13
The Apostle Who Failed

Luke 22:54–62

In Luke 22:54–62 the Bible states: "Then seizing him, they led him away and took him into the house of the high priest. Peter followed at a distance. But when they had kindled a fire in the middle of the courtyard and had sat down together, Peter sat down with them. A servant girl saw him seated there in the firelight. She looked closely at him and said, 'This man was with him.'

"But he denied it. 'Girl, I don't know him,' he said.

"A little later someone else saw him and said, 'You also are one of them.'

" 'Man, I am not!' Peter replied.

"About an hour later another asserted, 'Certainly this fellow was with him, for he is a Galilean.'

"Peter replied, 'Man, I don't know what you're talking about!' Just as he was speaking, the rooster crowed. The Lord turned and looked straight at Peter. Then Peter remembered the word the Lord had spoken to him: 'Before the rooster crows today, you will disown me three times.' And he went outside and wept bitterly" (NIV).

Recently while traveling through Florida, I saw some unusual things; but one thing stood out in my mind above all else. In the yards of some very beautiful houses, I saw vegetable gardens. Sometimes a garden constituted a fourth of the yard, sometimes half, sometimes the whole yard. I want you to know that people in small towns are not the only people who are trying to grow their own food. Everywhere, people who are trying to save money have gardens in their yards.

Not only are people trying to grow vegetables; they are also trying to grow meat. One morning while I was in a motel, I walked out onto the balcony, where I heard the strangest thing. In the midst of all the motels and the beautiful homes, I heard a rooster crowing.

When I heard that rooster crow in such unusual surroundings, I was amused. And then as I reflected on the experience, I remembered the biblical account of the crow of a rooster which was not amusing. For when Peter heard the cock crow, it was like the thunder of a thousand drums and the blast of a thousand bugles. To the average citizen in Jerusalem that morning, to hear the rooster crow meant nothing because it happened every day.

I have been in London; I have lived in New Orleans; I have visited in Rome; I have been in Johannesburg. In all of these places, I have never heard roosters crowing; but when I was in Jerusalem, I heard the roosters crow every morning. I suppose that ever since there has been a city called Jerusalem, the people have been awakened every morning by the cry of the rooster.

On that morning in the life of Peter, the crowing was a common sound heard by a hundred thousand people. To most people it meant nothing, but to Peter that common sound had a different meaning: It reminded Peter that he had failed.

The Surprise

In a way we are surprised by Peter's failure. If a person does not know the end of the gospel, or if he does not know the whole gospel story and is reading it for the first time, then he is probably surprised to realize that Peter failed. Matthew told us that when Jesus came to the coasts of Caesarea of Philippi, he asked his disciples, "Who do people say the Son of Man is?" (Matt. 16:13, NIV). And they all had various answers: John the Baptist, Elijah, or Jeremiah. Jesus repeated the question, and only Simon Peter answered: "You are the Christ, the Son of the living God" (v. 16, NIV). When Jesus sought a testimony from one of the disciples, it was usually Simon Peter who spoke. John told us that after Jesus had fed the five thousand, but then had refused to give them more bread, most of the disciples left. In fact, John stated it this way: "From this time many of his disciples turned back and no longer followed him.

" 'Do you want to leave too?' Jesus asked the Twelve.

" 'Simon Peter answered him, 'Lord, to whom shall we go? You have the words of eternal life. We believe and know that you are the Holy One of God' " (John 6:66–68, NIV).

Anytime that Jesus wanted a testimony, anytime that he wanted assurance that the disciples were going to stay with him to the end, it was always Peter who spoke. And for one who is reading the gospel for the first time, it would very likely be shocking to discover that at the fireside it was Peter who failed. Peter sinned; he failed. Why did Peter fail? Why do I fail? Why do you fail?

Some Reasons

I believe that a number of circumstances were involved in the failure of Simon Peter that night. He failed to allow the words of Jesus to control him. Jesus had repeatedly said that the disciples were to allow his words to control their lives. Jesus had often demonstrated what it could mean to have the word of God in control of one's life. Every time Jesus met the devil, he quoted Scripture. Through his example and his word, he was constantly trying to get the disciples to do what he was doing—allowing God's word to control every situation he faced. But the disciples did not allow the word of God to control their lives, and I think this is part of the reason why Simon Peter and the others failed.

Another reason Peter failed is that he did not pray. Jesus

tried to get him to pray by demonstrating the power of prayer. Early in the morning he would get up to pray. He talked to Peter about prayer and begged him to pray, but he would not.

Peter also failed that night because he was filled with pride. Proverbs says, "Pride goeth before destruction, and an haughty spirit before a fall." Longfellow must have had Proverbs 16:18 in front of him when he wrote these words: "Pride goeth forth on horseback grand and gay, But cometh back on foot, and begs its way." C. S. Lewis put it best when he wrote:

> There is one vice of which no man in the world is free; which every one in the world loathes when he sees it in someone else; and of which hardly any people, except Christians, ever imagine that they are guilty themselves. I have heard people admit that they are bad-tempered, or that they cannot keep their heads about girls or drink, or even that they are cowards. I do not think I have heard anyone who was not a Christian accuse himself of this vice . . . . The vice I am talking of is Pride or Self-Conceit. . . . Unchastity, anger, greed, drunkenness, and all that, mere fleabites in comparison: it was through Pride that the devil became the devil. Pride leads to every other vice . . . . In God you come up against something which is in every respect immeasurably superior to yourself. Unless you know God as that—and, therefore, know yourself as nothing in comparison—you do not know God at all. A proud man is always looking down on things and people. . . . as long as you are looking down, you cannot see something that is above you. That raises a terrible question. How is it that people who are . . . eaten up with Pride can say they believe in God and appear to themselves very religious? I am afraid it means they are worshipping an imaginary God. They . . . are really all the time imagining how He approves of them and thinks them far better

than ordinary people . . . . They pay a pennyworth of
imaginary humility to Him and get a pound's worth of
Pride toward their fellow-men . . . . Whenever we find
that our religious life is making us feel that we are . . .
better than someone else . . . we may be sure that we
are being acted on, not by God, but by the devil.[1]

C. S. Lewis says that the answer to pride is humility.
The first step in recovery is to realize that one is proud.
It is a big step and nothing whatever can be done before
that step is taken. If you think you are not proud, this, in
reality, means that you are very proud indeed. I believe
that this is why Peter failed, simply because he thought
that he could not fail. Simon Peter was always looking down;
he was never looking up. When all the others doubted their
faith, Simon Peter prematurely said, "No, everyone else
will fail, but not I. I will not fail. I will not fail." What
Peter was actually saying was that he was better than the
other men.

The Searching Gaze of Jesus

This thought on pride reminds me of one of Jesus' para-
bles. "Two men went up to the temple to pray, one a Pharisee
and the other a tax collector. The Pharisee stood up and
prayed about himself: 'God I thank you that I am not like
all other men—robbers, evildoers, adulterers—or even like
this tax collector. I fast twice a week, and give a tenth of
all my income'" (Luke 18:10–12, NIV). Every time I have
read that experience I have always thought that Jesus was
condemning the Pharisees. No doubt this is part of the lesson; however, Jesus was also saying to the apostles that if
they were not careful, that is the type of people they would
become. Jesus was warning his followers that religion can
become nothing more than sinful pride. Here is the danger
of doing good and right and of associating with people who
are doing right. If you are not careful, you will begin to
look down upon those who are doing wrong.

Simon Peter, James, John, and Andrew were talking with Jesus and doing good things because they were helping people and were doing everything that was right. Nevertheless, as Jesus looked into their hearts, he recognized their reasoning: "Why, we are good. Why, we are going with Jesus. We are doing everything that is right." Before long Jesus sensed that Peter, James, John, Andrew, and the rest of the apostles were doing good but, at the same time, were looking down on those who were doing wrong.

Jesus did not give the Sermon on the Mount to lost people. "Do not judge, or you too will be judged. For in the same way you judge others, you will be judged, and with the measure you use, it will be measured to you.

"Why do you look at the speck of sawdust in your brother's eye and pay no attention to the plank in your own eye?" (Matt. 7:1-3, NIV). No, Jesus did not give these words to lost people; he gave them to the twelve apostles because he understood that it would be so easy for his men who were doing good to look down upon those who were doing evil.

Jesus has called the apostles to live the good life but, at the same time, to redeem those who had forsaken God. Jesus understood that only a loving heart, empty of sinful pride, could reach a lost world.

Peter failed because of pride. Failure is not always bad; sometimes it can be a blessing in disguise. During the Pastors' Conference at the Southern Baptist Convention one year, Charles Colson gave his testimony as to how he had received Christ into his life. For you who have forgotten, Charles Colson was a very close aide to President Nixon and was one of the inner men involved in Watergate. He gave one of the most sincere testimonies I have ever heard. He openly and honestly discussed Watergate and his involvement. Do you realize that if there had never been a Watergate, Charles Colson might never have been won to the Lord. Perhaps he would never have been won to Christ if he had not failed. He quoted the article on pride by

C. S. Lewis that I referred to previously. He said: "That's what ruled in our hearts. We were building temples of power. And it wasn't until I failed and hit rock bottom that I looked up."

Thus, you see, failure is not always a detriment; sometimes it is a blessing in disguise. This was true for Simon Peter because only after he had failed did he fully realize who he was and that he could not make it in life without God's grace. Be assured that from that time on, Simon Peter spent most of his time looking to his heavenly Father for guidance in every situation.

Peter failed. He was imperfect, just like you and me. But in his case his failure was a blessing because, for the first time, he looked up. It could be that you have known failure. Maybe you have been filled with pride, as Peter was; but this does not mean that you are outside the reach of God's forgiveness. No man is so evil that he cannot be touched by God's grace. I challenge you to give that failure to God. Confess the sin that stands between you and God; turn (repent) from that sin; and receive the forgiveness of Christ. Like the apostle Peter, you can begin again. The book of Acts tells us that Simon Peter became a humble man who was mighty in God's power. This former failure became a blessing to thousands, and it can do the same for you. Open your heart to God and invite him in to be the boss in your life. Through the power of the Holy Spirit, he will begin to mold your character in Christlikeness.

14

Lift Your Head:
You Are Not Finished

Luke 24:13–35

In the Scriptures we find the following story: "That same day two of them were going to a village called Emmaus, about seven miles from Jerusalem. They were talking with each other about everything that had happened. As they talked and discussed these things with each other, Jesus himself came up and walked along with them; but they were kept from recognizing him.

"He asked them, 'What are you discussing together as you walk along?'

"They stood still, their faces downcast. One of them, named Cleopas, asked him, 'Are you the only one living in Jerusalem who doesn't know what things have happened there in these days?'

" 'What things?' he asked.

" 'About Jesus of Nazareth,' they replied. 'He was a prophet, powerful in word and deed before God and all the people. The chief priests and our rulers handed him over to be sentenced to death, and they crucified him; but we had hoped that he was the one who was going to redeem Israel. And what is more, it is the third day since all this took place. In addition, some of our women amazed us. They went to the tomb early this morning but didn't find his body. They came and told us that they had seen a vision of angels, who said he was alive. Then some of our companions went to the tomb and found it just as the women had said, but him they did not see.'

"He said to them, 'How foolish you are, and how slow

of heart that you do not believe all that the prophets have spoken! Did not the Christ have to suffer these things and then enter his glory?' And beginning with Moses and all the Prophets, he explained to them what was said in all the Scriptures concerning himself.

"As they approached the village to which they were going, Jesus acted as if he were going farther. But they urged him strongly, 'Stay with us, for it is nearly evening; the day is almost over.' So he went in to stay with them.

"When he was at the table with them, he took bread, gave thanks, broke it and began to give it to them. Then their eyes were opened and they recognized him, and he disappeared from their sight. They asked each other, 'Were not our hearts burning within us while he talked with us on the road and opened the Scriptures to us?'

"They got up and returned at once to Jerusalem. There they found the Eleven and those with them, assembled together and saying, 'It is true! The Lord has risen and has appeared to Simon.' Then the two told what had happened on the way, and how Jesus was recognized by them when he broke the bread" (Luke 24:13–35, NIV).

One day while I was visiting in a home, I noticed that over in a corner was a very sad-looking little boy. I commented to the mother that the child did not look very happy, and she responded: "Yes, he's down in the mouth." After the mother and I had talked a little while longer, she called her son to her and had him sit down next to her. She put her arm around him, brushed his hair, patted his shoulder, and said, "Son, lift your head. You're not finished yet!"

One aspect of Jesus' ministry was to seek people who had problems or tragedies or were in the midst of difficult times in order to say to them, "Listen, lift your heads. You're not finished yet!"

In this Scripture passage we see again this phase of the ministry of Jesus. He came to two men who were very sad and dejected, who, figuratively speaking, had their faces down on the ground; yet Jesus said to them, "Lift your heads. You are not finished yet!" These men seemingly had every right to be sad because they had experienced the death of someone they had loved and believed in. Anytime a person enters the personal realm of death, he always finds it very difficult to keep his head up. The hopes of these men had been shattered because they believed that Jesus was the Messiah, the one who was going to redeem Israel. Thus, it was natural that their faces were downcast.

Jesus did four things that day in an attempt to get these men to lift their heads. Just as Jesus did these things for those men that day, he still does these things for us today. First, in an attempt to get these men to look up rather than down, Jesus reached out to them; second, Jesus reasoned with them; third, Jesus related the Scripture; and last, but not least, Jesus revealed himself.

Jesus Reached Out

The Bible says that as they were walking together Jesus joined them and walked alongside. Literally, the Greek text says that the two men were walking and all at once, out of nowhere, a stranger appeared alongside to walk with them. First of all, Jesus reached out to them in their discussion.

The other day I received a phone call from a person in another state who had some problems which he wanted to discuss. He repeated the same thing many times; finally even realizing this himself he would say, "I know I am saying the same thing; I know I am saying the same thing. I know I must sound funny. I keep saying the same thing." In other words, he was talking; but his words were actually very few because he kept repeating essentially the same ideas and the same phrases.

In the Greek text, the idea presented states that these two men were "talking." Actually, they were saying the same thing over and over, probably something like "He's

dead! He's dead! He's dead!" This was the idea being exchanged between the two men when Jesus appeared to minister to them. Jesus reached out to them in their despair.
The Bible says that they were "still and downcast." The
King James says that they were "sad"; the Greek says that
they were "motionless." They were still and their faces were
downcast when Jesus appeared and said, "What is the matter?" But they could not look up because their grief was
so real; in fact, they could hardly speak.

Jesus reached out to them, not only in their disbelief but
also in their doubt. They looked at Jesus and said, "Are
you a stranger? Don't you know what has happened this
day in our city? Haven't you heard that Jesus, who was
mighty in deed, mighty in word, and mighty in his preaching, has been crucified by our rulers? And some women
have come and told us that angels have appeared unto them
and announced that he is alive. But when we went to his
tomb, we did not see him."

Do you ever feel that God is a thousand miles away? Has
there ever been a time when God has seemed as if he were
a billion miles away? Amid the experience of these men,
in their confusion, hurt, and pain, God seemed a thousand
miles away. Ironically, though, he was actually right next
to them, just as he is always with us. We must always remember that when life seems dark, purposeless, and without
hope, we cannot trust our feelings; instead, we must always
remember that the Word of God has taught that God is
always with his people, regardless of the circumstances.
Even when we cannot feel his presence, still he is there.
Jesus is always reaching out to us, trying to lift our heads.

Jesus Reasoned with Them

The Bible says that twice Jesus asked these men what
the matter was. Jesus was a great counselor. He already
knew their problem; he knew their hearts; he knew what
was hurting them on the inside. But Jesus also knew some-

thing else: They needed to talk about it. Finally, they poured out their hearts to God. God knows even before we go to him what the problem is; but he wants us to pour out that problem, to share that tragedy or that difficult experience. He knows that only as we share it with him is he able to commune with us and help. God wants you and me to come before his throne to bare our souls before him. The Father is always willing and ready to reason with us. No matter what the problem may be and no matter how small it may seem to you, do not be afraid or ashamed; go to God and say, "Lord, this is on my heart and I need help."

Jesus Related the Scripture

He reached out to them; he reasoned with them; and he related the Scripture to them. The Bible says that Jesus took the Old Testament, beginning with Moses and all the prophets, and explained to them that Christ must suffer and enter into his glory. When Jesus appeared to these two men, the Bible says that their eyes were "holden," which means that they could not understand who he was.

I have often wondered why in the beginning of this experience they could not recognize Jesus. I think this may be the answer: Jesus wanted them to understand that what had happened that week was not an accident but was God's divine plan. Had Jesus revealed himself to them instantly, they would have been so excited that they would not have taken the opportunity to study the Scripture and thus to understand that the cross had been God's plan. Jesus was also giving them an example so that in the days to come, when they shared their faith with others, they could also use the Scripture to say that Jesus died and rose again according to God's plan, as foretold by his prophets.

Jesus Revealed Himself

Jesus did something else that day to lift up their heads— he revealed himself to them. I want you to see something

that is very important—this revelation was by invitation
only. Jesus was about to walk on when they invited him
to come and have dinner with them. It was Jesus himself
who said, "I stand at the door, and knock: if any man hear
my voice, and open the door, I will come in . . . and will
sup with him, and he with me" (Rev. 3:20). They invited
Jesus to come in to have supper with them, and it was out
of this experience that they came to see who the Master
was. The Bible says that Jesus took the bread and broke
it, and it was as he broke the bread and gave it to them
that their eyes were opened so that they could see that
this was the Jesus whom they loved.

It is possible that these men had been with Jesus when
he fed the five thousand. They had probably heard Jesus
say after that experience: "I am the bread of life." I have
a feeling that this was one of Jesus' favorite sermons. I
personally believe that many times when Jesus was eating
with the apostles and his followers, he would break the bread
and, as he held it in his hands, would say: "Remember, I
am the bread of life. I am the one who gives strength. I
am your God."

After Jesus revealed himself to them, three things happened to those men: They had a "glow"; they had a "go";
and they had the "good news." The Bible says that their
hearts burned; they were on fire on the inside. The Bible
says that immediately they went back to Jerusalem and
told others that they had seen Jesus.

This very moment God wants to reach out to you and
to reason with you. This very moment God desires to relate
the Scripture to you and to reveal himself to you. God is
always reasoning with us; God is always relating the Scripture to us; God is always revealing himself to us. No matter
where you are, and no matter what your situation may be,
the loving Father is seeking to rule in your life. Even though
God may sometimes seem as if he is a thousand miles away,
he is not; he is really at your heart's door. If you are not

a Christian, then Christ wants to enter your heart so that he can make you his child. If you are a Christian but things seem very black, he wants to become real to you—so real that your heart will glow, that you will have a go, and that the good news will be upon your lips.

Just as God did it for them, he will do it for us. God loves us and is interested in us. When you walk down that road of despair and doubt, you must never forget that the God who ministered to those two disciples is the same God who seeks to minister to you. Lift your head: You are not finished yet!

Notes

CHAPTER 2

1. Norman Vincent Peale, *The Power of Positive Thinking* (Englewood Cliffs: Prentice-Hall, Inc., 1952), p. 68.
2. S. I. McMillen, *None of These Diseases* (Old Tappan: Fleming H. Revell Company, 1963), pp. 109–110, 111. Used by permission.

CHAPTER 3

1. McMillen, pp. 70–71.
2. Ibid., p. 71.
3. Ibid., p. 73.
4. William Sadler, *Practice of Psychiatry* (St. Louis: C. V. Mosley Co., 1953), p. 1008.

CHAPTER 4

1. Tim LaHaye, *Spirit-Controlled Temperament* (Wheaton: Tyndale House, 1973), p. 78. Used by permission.
2. McMillen, p. 115.
3. Ibid., pp. 73–74.
4. LaHaye, pp. 78–79.

CHAPTER 5

1. Joseph Fort Newton, "A Minister's Mail." *Reader's Digest Reprint* (October 1964).

CHAPTER 6

1. *Newsweek,* 8 January 1973.

CHAPTER 7

1. Bruce Narramore and Bill Counts, *Freedom from Guilt* (Santa Ana: Vision House, 1974), p. 38. Used by permission.
2. Maxwell Maltz, *Psycho-Cybernetics* (Englewood Cliffs: Prentice-Hall, Inc., 1960), pp. 2, 9. Used by permission.
3. Narramore and Counts, p. 40.
4. Words by John Newton, 1779.
5. Words by Isaac Watts, 1707.
6. R. R. Palmer and Joel Colton, *A History of the Modern World* (New York: Alfred A. Knopf, 1953), p. 11. Used by permission.
7. James D. Mallory, Jr., *The Kink and I* (Wheaton: Victor Books, 1973), pp. 33–34.
8. John R. W. Stott, *Basic Christianity* (Grand Rapids: William B. Eerdmans, 1972), p. 102.

CHAPTER 8

1. Maltz, p. 61.
2. Ibid., p. 67.

CHAPTER 9

1. Wesley H. Hager, *Conquering* (Grand Rapids: William B. Eerdmans, 1965), p. 11. Used by permission.
2. Ibid., p. 18.

CHAPTER 10

1. Nathaniel Hawthorne, *The Scarlet Letter* (New York: Dell Publishing Co., 1960), pp. 77, 84.
2. William Barclay, "The Gospel of John," *The Daily Study Bible* 2 (Philadelphia: Westminster Press, 1956), p. 4.

CHAPTER 11

1. Jack Taylor, *After the Spirit Comes . . .* (Nashville: Broadman Press, 1974), pp. 21–22.
2. Gary R. Collins, *Search for Reality* (Santa Ana: Vision House, 1969), p. 71.
3. Jay E. Adams, *Competent to Counsel* (Nutley, New Jersey: Presbyterian and Reformed Publishing Company, 1973), p. 9. Used by permission.
4. Ibid., pp. 29–30.
5. Ibid., pp. 31–34.

CHAPTER 12

1. Robert Schuller, *You Can Become the Person You Want to Be* (New York: Hawthorne Books, Inc., 1973), p. 73. Used by permission.
2. Hager, p. 12.
3. Ibid., p. 16.

CHAPTER 13

1. C. S. Lewis, *Mere Christianity* (New York: MacMillan, 1943), pp. 94, 96. Used by permission.

About the Author

Dr. Larry Wells Kennedy is pastor of the First Baptist Church of Laurel, Mississippi. Born in Louisiana, he was reared in Pensacola, Florida.

He was educated at Louisiana College (B.A.), New Orleans Baptist Theological Seminary (Th.M.), and Mississippi State University (M.A., Ph.D.). He began the ministry at nineteen and has pastored Manifest Baptist Church, Manifest Louisiana, Mantee Baptist Church, Mantee, Mississippi, and First Baptist Church, Amory, Mississippi, prior to becoming pastor at Laurel.

He is married to the former Martha F. Guinn of Jonesville, Louisiana. The Kennedys have two sons, Jon Stephen and Michael Scott.

Dr. and Mrs. Kennedy have received a number of academic and civic honors. Mrs. Kennedy was "Miss Louisiana College." Dr. Kennedy has preached in Europe, Africa, the Middle East, and South America. He is active in community and denominational life. He appears in the 1975 edition of *Outstanding Young Men of America.*